just imagine

Robina Beckles Willson
and Lyn Gray

Illustrations and Costumes by Lyn Gray

See instructions on page 14

First published in 1993 by BELAIR PUBLICATIONS LIMITED
Apex Business Centre, Boscombe Road, Dunstable, LU5 4RL, United Kingdom.

© 1993 Robina Beckles Willson and Lyn Gray
Reprinted 1998, 2001.

Series editor: Robyn Gordon
Design: Richard Souper
Photography: Kelvin Freeman
Illustrations and costumes: Lyn Gray

ISBN: 0 94788 223-5

Contents

Introduction

Many children become other people in their day-dreams and fantasies. Through drama, they can explore such imaginary roles and situations. In play and performance they learn more about their own voices and movements, as well as observing others. Shy and hesitant children will gain confidence; new talents will be released. When making simple costumes, masks and puppets, children will also develop ability in craft.

Ideas and stories throughout the curriculum can be brought to life by dramatic treatment. Children will remember characters and events from History, and understand more of the Geography in their world today when they have acted out past happenings and present situations. Maths concepts for younger children can be reinforced by acting number rhymes and games.

In this book, suggestions are given for all kinds of acting and dressing-up. The teacher or parent can adapt them to suit the children and the occasion. Staging will often need to be flexible. Work may be done in individual spaces or in the round, as well as on raised blocks, platforms and stages.

First concentrate on mime and movement, developing listening skills and concentration. Use of the voice is more difficult for the child, so can be worked in gradually. In mime pieces, children may begin to add their own words spontaneously.

Whenever possible, arrange links with professional actors, who might visit the school, or be visited at workshops and theatres. In any case, children will begin to appreciate and assess performances as soon as they watch school plays in classrooms and assemblies.

Enjoying drama in all its forms will improve the quality of children's learning and help them to become lively and confident individuals.

R.B.W. and L.G.

Some Basic and Easy Activities

Warm-up
● Walk in a circle, as if limping, old, frightened, being followed.
● Practise falls, as if ill, tripping, fainting, wounded; each child in his own space.
● Mime actions of everyday life: sitting, crouching, kneeling, sweeping, folding, dressing.

Control
Establish and try out agreed signs, meaning Stop, Freeze, Go.

Stillness and Silence as Relaxation
● Imagine being a rag doll; an empty sack lying on the ground; flopping as if on a soft bed.
● Teacher or children could try lifting arms or legs, to check that they are relaxed.

Simple Signals
● Try different kinds of waving.
● Practise policeman's signals: Stop, Go, Beckoning.
● Use various expressions: smiling, frowning, looking puzzled.

Machine Movements (for groups of three or four)
● Each group devises a machine, using their heads, bodies, arms and legs. Demonstrate to the others.
● All machines could work together, stopping to order, going fast or in slow motion. Sounds of humming, hissing and popping can be added.

Rhythmic Chanting
Such rhymes as 'This old man', and 'Jeremiah Obadiah, puff, puff, puff...'

Telephone Chats
In pairs, with yoghurt pots and string as telephones, children practise, then perform, conversations to the class. Give hints, if needed: invitations, arrangements, complaints, thanks.

Telephone Game
The class and the teacher make a circle. The teacher has a toy telephone and another is passed round the circle while she closes her eyes. When she says 'Stop', she holds a short conversation with the child holding the telephone.

Parades and Processions

Children can respond dramatically to music by making parades with mime and movement.

Clear as much space as possible in the classroom, or hall, or go outside. Prepare the music beforehand (for example, storm music for the Monsters). Let the children be as free as is practicable. When space is limited, split the class in two, and let the 'audience' sit in the middle and comment on the parade afterwards; then change around.

March of the Monsters (loud, stormy music)
Discuss and try out lumbering movements and fearsome faces; or use masks. Perhaps divide the class into monsters and those being chased, acting as though frightened. Try out signs of alarm.

The children can resolve the outcome of the encounter. Either the monsters each catch a child, or those threatened catch monsters and lead them away triumphantly.

Circus Parade (a quick march)
Children suggest and work out roles to be played. When everyone has a part, the parade begins. Suggestions: **Ring Master,** with whip; **Band,** miming drum, cymbals, trumpet, horn, trombone; **Jugglers, Clowns,** falling and fooling as human wheelbarrows; **Strong man,** with weights; **Trick Cyclists**; **Trapeze artists,** doing cartwheels or somersaults.

Caribbean Carnival Procession (a Calypso song)
Have players of pretend drums, with hands or sticks; scratch scrapers; tap sticks together; shake maraccas, or home-made percussion instruments. You could also have banners on sticks to thump on the ground in rhythm. Dancers could stamp and clap in time.

American Cheerleaders ('The Star-Spangled Banner')
At some football and basketball matches, cheerleaders march around the pitch ahead of a band, to encourage their teams. Pom-pom girls have fluffy pom-poms on their hands, to wave about. Some twirl batons, passing them from one hand to the other. Some dance about, swinging their legs, twisting shoulders and nodding heads, in time to the music. The rest of the class can play in the band.

Australian Songlines (Aboriginal music)
The whole class hums, and children chant out their contributions.
They go Walkabout, like the Australian Aborigines in the Outback, following ancient trails. In turns, they sing a naming game as they walk round in a circle. 'I am the earth. I am a river. I am a mountain. I am a lake. I am a bridge. I am a gum tree. I am the grass. I am a wild flower. I am the sun. I am the moon. I am a star. I am a rock. I am the rain. I am the wind. I am the storm.'

Goorialla, the Sea-serpent's Dance
Aboriginal stories tell of Dreamtime, when the world began, and men sang magic songs and carried firesticks through the dark forests. Some men changed into the creatures who live in Australia today. Make a procession, led by Goorialla, the sea-serpent, of animals and birds, moving in their distinctive ways to Aboriginal music.
First let everyone try out movements, then choose their parts. The giant sea-serpent can be two children crawling along, the back one holding the other round the waist. Snakes slither. Kangaroos jump with big back legs. Crocodiles swim and snap huge mouths made with hands and arms opening and closing from the elbows. Bees fly and buzz. Koala bears clamber and climb. Pelicans waddle and dip their heads. Parrots flutter and peck. Kookaburras laugh and fly. Lizards make darting runs, then lie still.

Instructions for Clowns on page 12

Other ideas to develop

Children can make their own suggestions for other groupings, with or without music, such as:

- Indian festival dancers.

- A triumphant football team, marching around a stadium.

- The Pied Piper leading rats away from Hamelin, then all the children except one.

- An Easter bonnet parade, with all sorts of hats.

- Flights of birds: work out movements for flying with arms or wings (see page 27 onwards).

- Marching in character when dressed up, as King, Queen, Judge, Gypsy, Pirate, Witch, Ghost, Soldier. (See Dressing-up section, page 10 onwards.)

- See also the use of processions in the Nativity play (page 60) and 'Goodbye to a Greedy Dragon' (page 65).

Drama Games

All these suggestions can be adapted to suit different ages and numbers. To give variety and develop the games, use ideas from the class.

MOVEMENT

Fish of the Sea
The children make up groups, each with the name of a fish. The teacher, as the Sea, walks about, calling them to follow: 'The Sea wants the shrimps. The Sea wants the cod...'. When they are all gathered, the Sea says 'I am calm': children move on tiptoe, gliding. 'I am rough': children hop. 'I am choppy': children skip. 'I am stormy': children run, waving their arms about.

Grandmother's Footsteps
All the class makes a line, except one, who, as Grandmother, goes to the other end of the room with her back to them. On the word 'Go', the children creep towards Grandmother, who turns round if she hears a movement, sending that player back to the starting line. The winner is the first to touch Grandmother, and takes her place.

Musical Statues
Everyone dances round in own space to the music until it stops. Then all the children freeze and hold their poses until the music starts again. Anyone who wobbles or moves is out. The last one left is the winner.

MIMING

Changeable Chairs
A child sits on a chair, and is secretly told by the teacher that it is hot, smelly, slippery, has wet paint, a drawing pin or glue on it, a snake on its leg. The watching class guesses what is being acted, and the one who guesses correctly has the next turn.

What am I Playing?
Teacher mimes the playing of a musical instrument, which can then be copied by everyone, when it is guessed correctly: piano, recorder, guitar, organ, drum, violin, flute, 'cello, clarinet, double bass.

Who am I?
A child acts as a pop-singer, policeman, postman, wrestler, footballer, gardener, bus driver, window cleaner. The class guesses, and the one who is right has the next turn.

What is it?
A small towel is given to a child and he acts with it, pretending it is a cat, a baby, a mat, a scarf, a tablecloth, an Indian turban, an apron, a skateboard, and much else, as the other children make guesses. This game provides good entertainment and gives opportunity for a lot of children to take part.

What Animal is this?
Children silently act as animals, and other players try to identify them: tiger - paces; bull - paws the ground; monkey - jumps and swings with tail; kangaroo - bounds; crocodile - swims and snaps mouth; cat - washes face, curls up; gorilla - beats chest; dog - begs; rabbit - bunny-hops; beaver - swims and nibbles.

See 'Fish of the Sea' on facing page

Joke acting in pairs

Work out tricky situations together, then perform and ask for guesses. Some examples which can be given secretly to start children off: teaching someone to swim; escaping from a wasp; trying to cut the hair of a wriggling child; cowboy trying to rope a bucking horse; giving medicine to a cat; feeding a baby with a spoon.

GAMES WITH DISGUISED VOICES

Grunt, Piggy, Grunt

Children sit in a circle. One blindfolded child is turned about inside the circle, then comes and sits on a knee and says, 'Grunt, Piggy, grunt'. If she guesses correctly who is grunting, that child is blindfolded next.

Betty's Questions

The players stand in a ring, with one in the middle blindfolded and holding a walking stick. They dance around this Blindfold Betty until she knocks three times on the floor. Then they stand still as she points her stick at a child, who grasps it. He has to answer three questions from her, with a squeak for 'Yes', and a groan for 'No'. If she guesses who it is, they change places.

Where are you, Adam?

The children run about, and one who is blindfolded has to catch somebody. Then she (if a girl) says 'Where are you, Adam?' and he/she answers in a disguised voice, 'Here I am, Eve.' (Or the other way around 'Where are you Eve?' 'Here I am, Adam.') If she recognises who it is, he takes her place.

Dressing Up

The following quick and easy ideas will help children to imagine themselves as different characters in varied roles.

Wherever possible, paper, card and household articles have been chosen in preference to bought fabrics, allowing the children to be involved in much of the making. The results should be cheap and immediate.

It is rarely feasible for every child to have a complete costume, but with the addition of one or two articles, for example a tail or a hat, a whole character can be suggested. It is with this in mind that this chapter is divided up, each part concentrating on a different area of the body.

Measurements may need to be adapted to individual children.

HATS AND HEADDRESSES

using a simple headscarf

Nativity

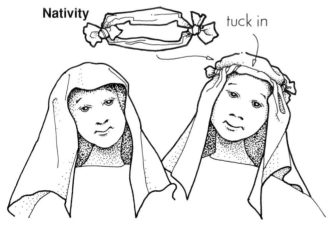

tuck in

Lay the flat scarf over the head as shown. Tie two stretch pop socks together, making a circle to secure the scarf in place. The front of the scarf can be lifted and tucked into the band.

Pirate

Fold a scarf into a triangle. Positioning it low on the forehead, tie the scarf to one side behind the ear.

Nurse

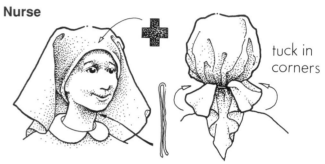

tuck in corners

Fold a starched table napkin into a triangle and secure firmly round the head with a safety pin or hairgrip at the nape of the neck, **or,** gather the napkin at the back into a thick elastic band, tucking the outer corners into the band.

1940's Worker

Fold a scarf into a triangle. Positioning the corners to the front, tie securely and tuck the ends in.

Peasant

secure with double–sided adhesive tape if necessary

Fold a small scarf into a triangle and tie at the back of the head. Fold a large scarf into a triangle and drape over the first scarf.

Turban Shape
using a child's long knitted scarf

Position the scarf round the back of the head. Cross over the ends in front and tuck in.

Or, using 2metres (80in) of tubular stockinette roll (sold for polishing)

Place the centre of the strip over the head. Cross over at the back and bring the ends forward, crossing over at the front. Cross once more at the back and lastly the front. Tuck the ends in.

Simple Medieval Headcovering

tuck in round face

Cut a length of tubular stockinette roll (sold for polishing). Pull it over the head and drape round the shoulders.

Padded Medieval Hat

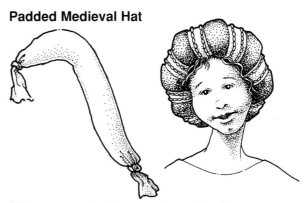

Either use a stocking or cut one leg from a pair of tights. Tie a knot approximately 15cm (6in) from the toe.
Stuff the leg with wadding/shredded paper and tie a second knot at the other end.
Fit round the child's head and tie both ends together.
Suggested decoration - ribbon/crêpe/ Christmas decorations.

Chinese Hat
(photograph on page 45)

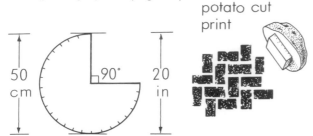

potato cut print

Cut a circle of paper diameter 50cm (20in). Remove one quarter and make 1cm (½in) cuts into the circumference.
If wished, print a woven pattern using a cut potato.

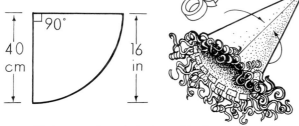

double-sided adhesive tape

Construct the hat folding the bottom edge inwards. Secure a ribbon of crêpe paper inside the point.

Witch's Hat

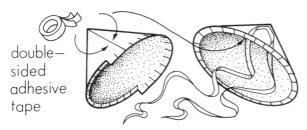

Cut a quarter circle from black paper radius 40cm (16in). Construct the hat.
Curl long strips of paper over a metal ruler (method, see page 16) and attach inside the bottom edge.

Princess Hat

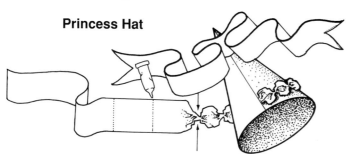

Follow the instructions for the witch's hat. Decorate with toilet paper. Apply glue to the perforations and gather.
Glue this border round the bottom edge and a strip of toilet paper to the back of the hat as shown.

Clown Hat
(photograph on page 7)

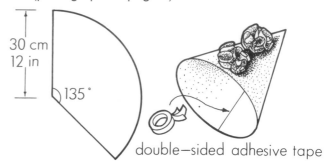

double-sided adhesive tape

Cut the above segment of a circle radius 30cm (12in). Construct the hat.
Attach pom-poms to hat, clothes or shoes with double-sided adhesive tape (for instructions see page 26).

Clown's Neck Ruff (line drawing)

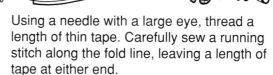

Cut a 150cm (60in) length of crêpe paper. Split lengthways down the centre and place the two pieces together. Make a fold line along the centre.

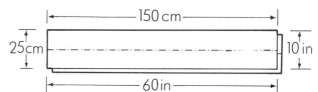

Using a needle with a large eye, thread a length of thin tape. Carefully sew a running stitch along the fold line, leaving a length of tape at either end.
Gather crêpe and separate the layers.
Tie the ruff round neck.

Flower Head

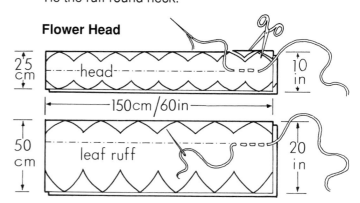

Use the measurements given and follow the instructions for the clown ruff. The leaf ruff can be tied round the waist as a skirt.

Crowns
(photograph on page 43)

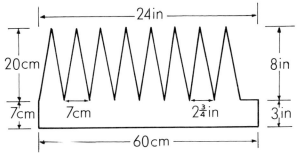

Draft and cut the crown using the measurements given. Fit the crown and secure.

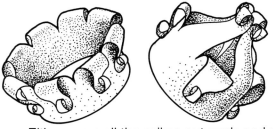

Either curve all the spikes outwards and glue on to the headband.
Or, position four spikes outwards and four spikes over the head. Suggested decorations: sweet papers, fruit gums, foil covered chocolate coins.
Toilet paper for wimple.

Paper Chain Ruff

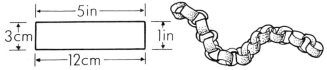

Construct the chain and place round neck. Secure with an extra link.

Bonnets
(photograph on page 41)

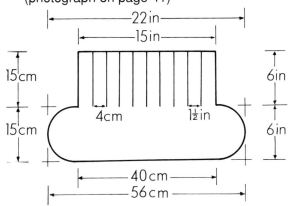

Draft and cut the bonnet, using the measurements given.

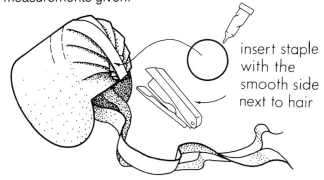

insert staple with the smooth side next to hair

Gather strips together and staple in place. A paper circle can be positioned over the back to neaten. Secure a ribbon of crêpe paper inside the top of the bonnet.
Suggested decorations: doilies, crêpe paper, tissue paper, paper ribbon, Christmas crêpe streamers (the type gathered down the centre with stitching).

Brimmed Hat
(photograph on page 2)

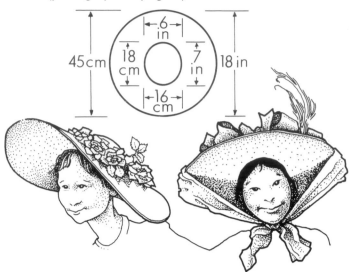

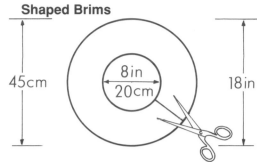

Cut a circle of card or corrugated cardboard, diameter 45cm (18in). Remove an oval 18cmx16cm (7inx6in) from the centre. Heavy card will produce a rigid brim; thinner card will give a softer line.

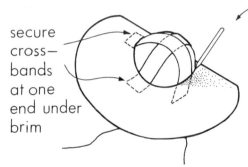

secure cross—bands at one end under brim

fit, mark and then secure at the other end

The brim will fit more securely with the addition of crossbands. These should be cut approximately 5cmx32cm (2inx13in) and fitted for each individual.

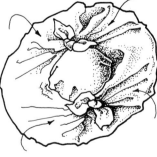

The brim can be covered by draping a large scarf over the head and placing the brim on top. Lift the four corners of the scarf over the top of the brim and tie.
Suggested decorations; scarves, artificial flowers, dried flowers, feathers, ribbon, crêpe paper, tissue paper.

Shaped Brims

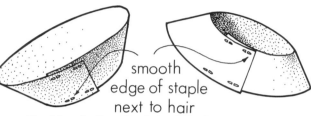

Cut a circle of card or corrugated cardboard, diameter 45cm (18in). Remove a circle, diameter 20cm (8in). Cut a line through the brim.

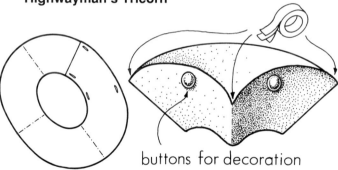

smooth edge of staple next to hair

Decide whether the brim is to turn up or down, then overlap the cut edges and fit to the child. Mark, remove and staple brim.

Highwayman's Tricorn

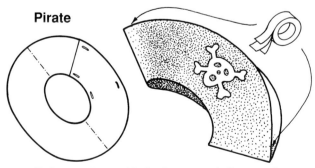

buttons for decoration

Cut an upturned brim from card. Score along the three fold lines shown. Bend the brim to make three corners which can be held in place with double-sided adhesive tape. Staple to fit.

Pirate

Cut an upturned brim from card. Score along the two fold lines shown. Bend the brim to make two creases which can be held in place with double-sided adhesive tape.
Apply the skull and crossbones. Staple to fit.

Paper Plate Hat
(photograph on page 13)

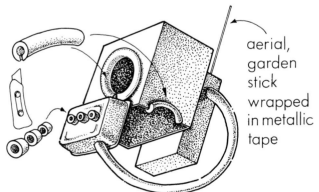

A simple hat can be made by securing a ribbon to the underside of a paper plate. Decorate and tie under the chin.

Spaceman's Helmet
(photograph on page 35)

aerial, garden stick wrapped in metallic tape

The basic helmet is a box a little larger than a child's head with a circle removed for the face. Cut off the bottom of the box and shape the two sides so that they fit round the shoulders. The corners of the box can be reinforced with masking tape. Paint the box white.
Using cereal packets/ice cream cartons, add a front and back pack.
Expanded foam pipe wrap available from D.I.Y. stores can be used for air pipes, edging and control knobs.

Soldier's Hat
(photograph on page 23)

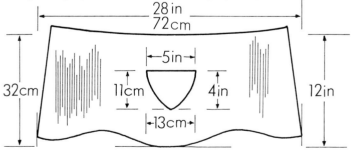

secure inside flowerpot holes

7in
18cm

Choose a black plastic flowerpot larger than the child's head. Pad the bottom of the pot with crumpled paper. Cut a peak shape as shown and secure inside the rim.
Suggested decorations: dressing-gown cord, braid, feathers, gold doilies and foil-covered chocolate coins.

Knight's Helmet
(photographed with armour on page 19)

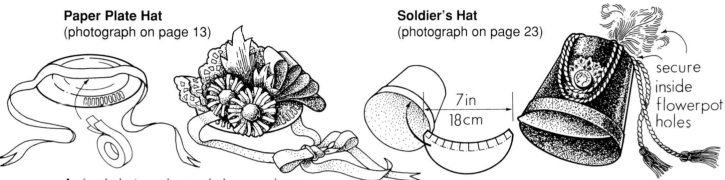

28 in
72 cm
5 in
32cm   11cm   4 in   12in
13cm

Cut out the helmet from corrugated cardboard, using the measurements given. The ridges should run vertically up and down the helmet. Spray the surface with silver paint. Check the fit of the helmet and staple together at the back with the smooth edge of the staple next to the hair.
Decorate with a feather duster.

WIGS AND HAIRPIECES

Judge's Wig

This big wig is very effective. Use a double page of a large daily newspaper.
Fold as shown so that the final strip has eight layers. Cut the strip as above.
Unwrap the paper with care to prevent tearing, and drape over the head.

Judge's Necktie

Cut a neckband from white crêpe paper, 8cmx40cm (3inx16in). Fold in half lengthways.
Cut two strips 4cmx30cm (1½inx12in). Glue each strip to form a loop which is threaded on to the neckband.
Secure the band at the back of the neck with masking tape or a paper clip.

Ringlets

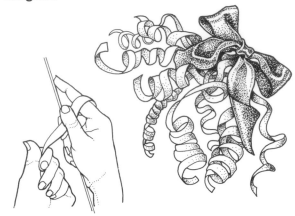

Cut strips of brown gummed paper and/or curling paper ribbon sold for decorating gifts. Holding each strip at the angle shown, pull firmly over a metal edge to produce the ringlet curl.
Gather curled strips together and either glue to a hat or attach to a hairband.

Plaits and Bunches

'Pantomime' plaits and bunches can be made from garden raffia. Cut a quantity of raffia to the required length and bind together at the top. Either leave loose or plait and bind near the bottom. Attach hairpieces to a hat or a hairband.

Bows

Quick and cheap bows can be made from wide paper ribbon sold at florists' shops.

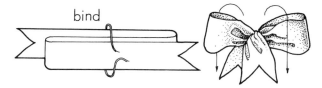

Fold a length of ribbon into three layers as shown, and bind the centre very tightly with thin wire or thread. Pull both ends of the ribbon downwards.

COLLARS

These collars can be cut from thin paper, crêpe paper, Vilene interfacing, or felt, depending on required durability. It should be remembered, however, that the cut edge of paper can be uncomfortable next to the skin. All collars are attached to clothes with double-sided adhesive tape.

Round Collar

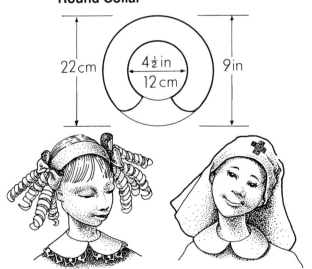

Make a paper pattern: cut a circle diameter 22cm (9in). Remove a circle for the neck, diameter 12cm (4½ in). Trim the opening back as shown.
Check the shape of the paper pattern on the child. Place the pattern on to the chosen material and cut out the collar.
A lace collar can be cut from a paper doily or a combination of iron-on Vilene interfacing and doilies.

Puritan Collar

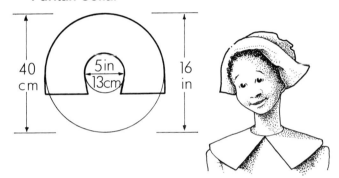

Make a paper pattern: draft a large circle diameter 40cm (16in). Draft a smaller circle diameter 13cm (5in). Using the two circles, draft and cut the collar shape as shown. Check the paper pattern on the child. Place the pattern on to the chosen material and cut out the collar.

Cavalier Collar

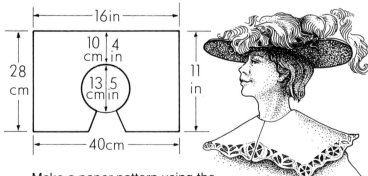

Make a paper pattern using the measurements given. Fit the pattern to the child and then cut out the collar from the chosen material. Trim with doily pieces. Wear back to front for an Edwardian collar (see photograph above).

17

CAPES AND TABARDS

Small Capes

These may be cut from Vilene interfacing or felt.

felt

decorated
vilene
interfacing

Make a paper pattern: cut a circle diameter 60cm (24in). Remove a circle for the neck, diameter 13cm (5in). Trim back the opening of the cape as shown. Check the paper pattern on the child. Place the pattern on the chosen material and cut out.

Pointed Medieval/Jester Cape

As above, removing triangles as shown.

Egyptian Collar

Decorate the basic cape with straws, coloured card, foil and/or pulses. Wear with the opening down the back.

Royal Cape
(photograph on page 21)

Make a paper pattern using the measurements given. Cut the final cape out of Terylene wadding.
Decorate the cape with narrow strips of black felt and complete with a bow at the neck.

'Feather' Boa

This boa utilises shredded paper which is thrown away by offices. If available, the folded shreds look best and are easier to manage.

Cut a strip of white crêpe paper approx. 18cm (7in) wide by the required length. Fold in half along the length and fringe as shown.

Open up the strip and glue as much shredded paper as possible along the centre of both sides of the crêpe strip.

Simple Tabard

A simple way of making a cloth tabard is to join a pair of pillowcases with two safety pins as shown. Turn the pillowcases over so that the pins no longer show.
This tabard can be worn loose or with a tie.

18

KNIGHT'S ARMOUR
(Instructions for helmet on page 15)

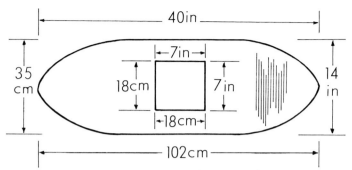

Using the measurements given, cut the armour from corrugated cardboard, with the ridges running across the width. Remove a square for the head.

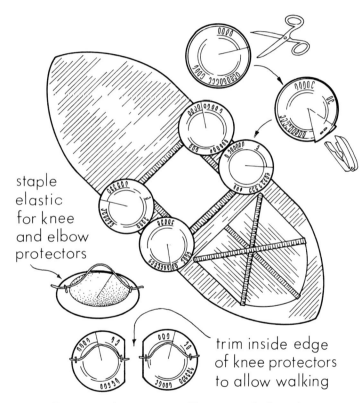

staple elastic for knee and elbow protectors

trim inside edge of knee protectors to allow walking

Decorate the armour with corrugated card as shown. Take four small paper plates and make a cut into the centre of each. Overlap the cut edges and staple in place. Spray the armour and plates with silver paint. Position the plates over the shoulders and staple on to the armour.

With the addition of elastic, further plates can be used for knee and elbow protectors.

Or, for a glossier metallic finish, paste a patchwork of cooking foil on to the unridged surface of the cardboard.

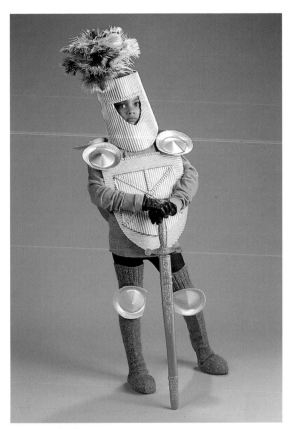

Knight in Armour

Simple Stiff Tabard

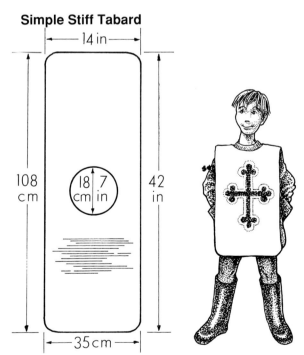

Using the measurements given, cut the tabard from corrugated cardboard with the ridges running across the width. Remove a circle for the head.

Words, symbols or pictures can be pasted, printed or painted on to the flat surface, in which case the smooth side of the cardboard should be uppermost.

19

CLOAKS

The cloaks on these two pages are fun to make and wear, but being made of paper or thin plastic, their life is short.

Royal Cloak

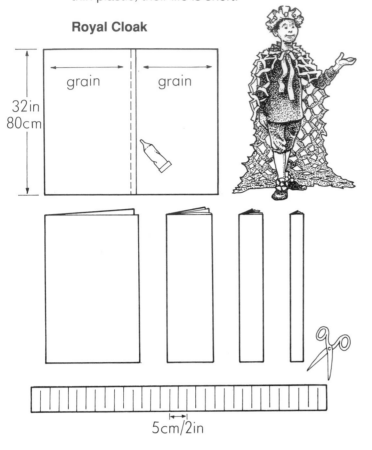

Take a roll of purple crêpe paper approx. width 50cm (20in) and cut two 80cm (32in) lengths. Glue the lengths together forming a double width. Fold along the length four times, as accurately as possible; the final strip should have sixteen layers.
Make cuts at 5cm (2in) intervals along both sides of the strip, as shown. Carefully unfold the crêpe paper and gently pull the cloak open.

Cut a ribbon of crêpe paper width 4cm (1½in) wide, length 150cm (60in). With the glued seam running down the centre back, gather up the top of the cloak and staple on to the ribbon as shown.
Single lengths of crêpe paper can be folded and cut separately, then stapled together to make a cloak of any size.

Dracula/Witch's Cloak

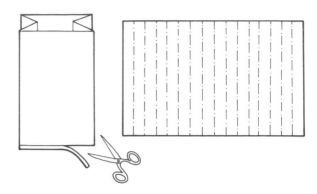

Cut the sealed bottom off a black dustbin liner. Open the liner flat by cutting up the side, and then follow the instructions for the royal cloak by folding the liner four times and making cuts along both edges of the folded strip.
Cut a ribbon of black crêpe paper 4cm (1½in) wide, length 150cm (60in). Complete the cloak by threading the ribbon down one side of the liner; this makes a wider cloak encircling the child more than the royal cloak (which hangs down the child's back).

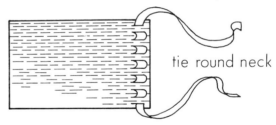

tie round neck

All-Purpose Decorative Strip

This has been included here as it is made in the same way as the previous cloaks. The strip is ideal for improvisation, as it can become anything from a scarf to foliage for a tree (see photograph opposite).

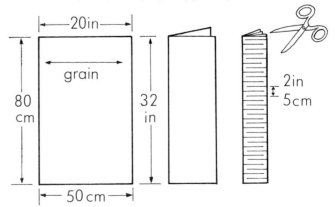

Cut a length of crêpe paper 80cm (32in). Fold twice along the length and cut as shown. Unfold carefully.

King and Witch's cloaks, together with a tree made from the all-purpose decorative strip (instructions on facing page)

Paper Chain Cloak

This cloak can be made to any size. To be fully practical, it is important that the links are secure. A group of children could be involved with the making, in which case brown gummed parcel tape would be a good choice of material. However, the links may be made of any coloured paper, providing each join is fixed with strong glue/staples/double-sided adhesive tape.

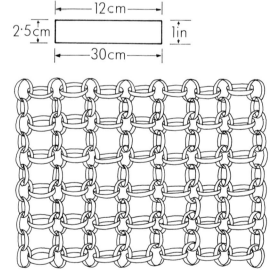

Each link should be approx 2.5cmx30cm (1in x 12in). Make eight chains of eleven links. Lay the chains in vertical rows on the floor and link together every other link as shown. The child wearing the cloak may put her/his head through any gap between the links.

ADAPTING CLOTHES

The starting point for many costumes has to be the clothes that the children have themselves, such as jeans, games wear, tracksuit, T-shirt, tights, leotards.

One simple way to transform everyday wear into something special is to apply a design of adhesive backed plastic. This is sold in plain and patterned colours in large DIY stores.

Cut out the shapes that you want; remove the backing and stick the plastic on to the garment. At a later stage the plastic can be peeled off without spoiling the fabric beneath.

Adhesive backed plastic may also be used to suggest the markings of animals.

A decorated T-shirt combined with a mask can complete a transformation.

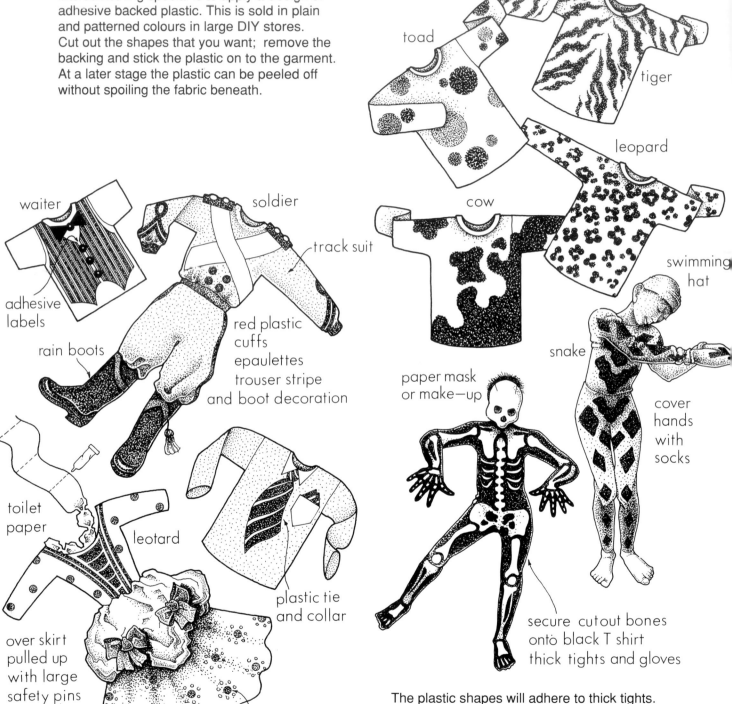

toad

tiger

leopard

cow

swimming hat

snake

waiter

adhesive labels

rain boots

soldier

track suit

red plastic cuffs epaulettes trouser stripe and boot decoration

paper mask or make—up

cover hands with socks

toilet paper

leotard

plastic tie and collar

over skirt pulled up with large safety pins covered with bows

adhesive labels

secure cutout bones onto black T shirt thick tights and gloves

The effect should be bright, and larger than life.

The plastic shapes will adhere to thick tights. However, they will be more secure with the addition of double-sided adhesive tape and should be applied whilst the tights are being worn. If the decorated tights are to be taken off and used again, it may be worth tacking the plastic shapes on with thread.

 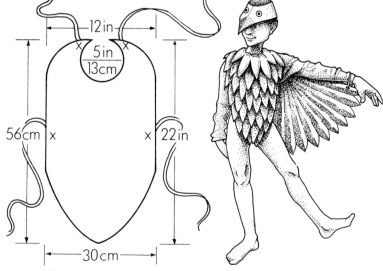

Ghost and Soldier, with adhesive-backed plastic used to decorate plain T-shirt and leggings

Ghosts

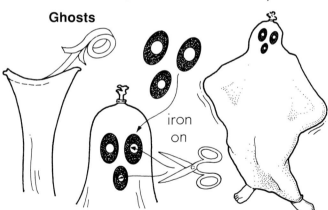

Cut a length of tubular stockinette (sold for polishing) one and half times the height of the child. Iron one end, stretching slightly, and stick together using double-sided adhesive tape between the layers. Gather the sealed end together with an elastic band.

Pull the stockinette over the child until the sealed end fits to the head. With the child's eyes closed, carefully mark the position of the eyes and mouth and remove the stockinette.

Using iron-on black Vilene interfacing, cut out shapes for the eyes and mouth as shown. Iron shapes on to the marked stockinette and finally cut out the eye and mouth holes.

Body Disguise
(photograph on page 29)

This bib can be cut out of Vilene interfacing or felt. It is then covered with textured materials to suggest feathers or fur depending on the chosen creature.

If wished, make a paper pattern from the measurements given and check for size against the child. Cut the bib from the chosen material and attach tapes at each cross mark to tie behind the neck and waist.

(Hat instructions are on page 34.)

HANDS, CLAWS AND FEET

Long Nails and Claws

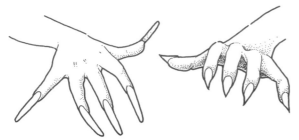

Nails and claws can be cut out of coloured paper and secured directly on top of the child's nails with small pieces of Blu-Tack.

Paws

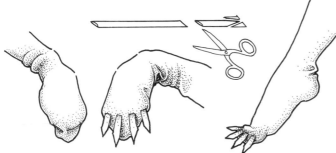

Paws are best suggested by socks of a suitable colour worn on both hands and feet. If claws are needed, flatten a paper drinking straw and cut into short lengths.
Trim one end into a point and position on to the sock using double-sided adhesive tape. Shade the straight end of the straw with a crayon to blend the claw into the sock.

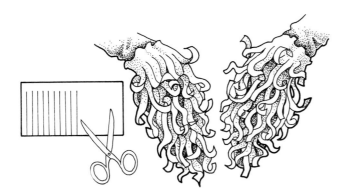

Old socks can provide the base for furry paws. Cut short strips of crêpe paper of a suitable colour, and fringe as shown.
Gently stretch the fringing over a metal edge to curl lightly. Place a hand inside the sock, and, starting at the toe, secure the fringing in layers - preferably using a rubber-based glue.

Aquatic Feet and Hands

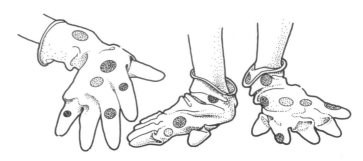

Rubber gloves look effective on the feet as well as the hands. They can be used for aquatic birds, frogs or toads, and can be decorated with adhesive labels.

Webbed Feet

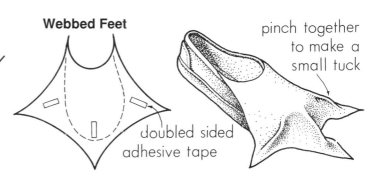

pinch together to make a small tuck

doubled sided adhesive tape

Webbed feet can be cut out of felt and secured on to shoes with double-sided adhesive tape. Using the sole as a guide for size, draft and cut a webbed shape as shown. Stick three small strips of double-sided adhesive tape on the back of the felt to make three neat tucks in line with the three points. Fit over the shoe front.

Hooves

(for hands only)

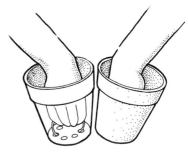

Find a pair of small black plastic flowerpots. Cut two lengths of string and thread through two holes at the base of the flowerpots as shown. Tie into a loop and pull through inside the pot. Stretching their sleeves down over their hands, the children wear the hooves by holding on to the string loops. Drum together for hoof sound effects.

From left to right - buckled and pom-pom shoes, feathered and webbed feet, rosette shoes, and lace decorated boots (instructions on these two pages and page 26)

Large Feathered Feet

Rain boots provide the base for these feathered legs.

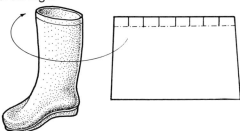

First make two boot covers on which to stick the texture. These may be cut from Vilene interfacing or paper and need to be wide enough to encircle the boot and long enough to reach the foot. Add extra length along the top edge to bend over and secure inside the boot with double-sided adhesive tape.

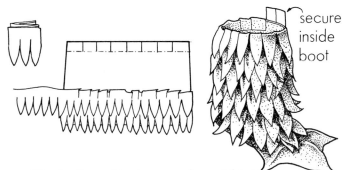

secure inside boot

The feathered texture can be cut from newspaper/crêpe/tissue etc. Cut long feather strips and glue in layers on to the cover, starting from the bottom.
Complete the boot with a webbed foot if required (see opposite).

Large Furry Feet

(photograph page 53)
Rain boots provide the base for these furry feet. Cut two boot covers, following the instructions for the feathered feet. Allow extra length along the top edge of the cover to bend over and secure inside the boot once the decoration is complete.

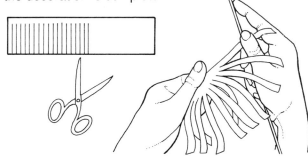

Cut strips of crêpe paper of the required colour and fringe as shown. Gently stretch the fringing over a metal edge to curl lightly.

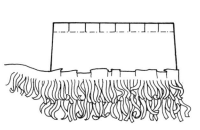

Glue the fringed strips in layers on to the cover starting from the bottom. Secure the cover inside the boot with double-sided adhesive tape.

Paper Chain Cuffs

These match the ruffs on page 13

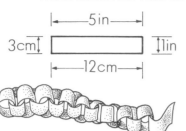

Construct the chain and place round the wrist, securing with an extra link.

Plain and Lace Cuffs

Cuffs can be cut from paper, Vilene interfacing or felt. Secure to the end of the sleeve with double-sided adhesive tape.

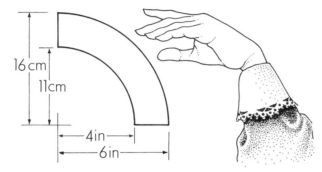

The cuff is constructed from a quarter segment of a circle. The inner radius is 11cm (4in). The outer radius is 16cm (6in). A lace cuff can be cut from a combination of iron-on Vilene interfacing and doilies.

Boot Decorations

(photograph on page 25)
Use the same materials as above.

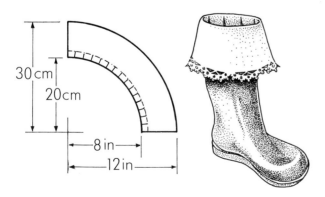

The decoration is constructed from a quarter segment of a circle. The inner radius is 20cm (8in). The outer radius is 30cm (12in). Cut fixing tabs which tuck inside a rain boot. Secure with double-sided adhesive tape.

Shoe Decorations

(photograph on page 25)
These are simple ideas to decorate or disguise school/gym shoes. They can be secured with double-sided adhesive tape.

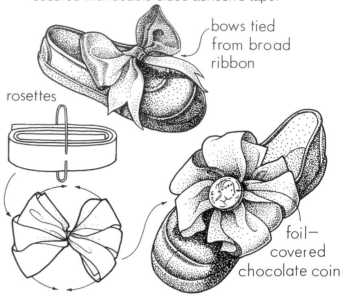

Rosettes can be made from a folded length of ribbon bound tightly round the centre with thin wire or thread. Pull the folded ribbon ends apart to shape the rosette.

Pom-poms are particularly useful for decorating clowns.

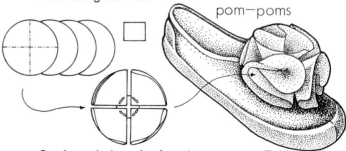

Cut four circles of crêpe/tissue paper. Fold each circle into a quarter, and staple on to a small square of card.
Carefully open up each paper circle.

Buckles can be placed on shoes or boots.

Cut the tongue and strap from felt to match the colour of the shoe. The buckle can be cut from thick card and covered with self-adhesive metallic strip. Secure both ends of the strap to the shoe.

Eye mask instructions on page 34

WINGS

Butterfly Wings

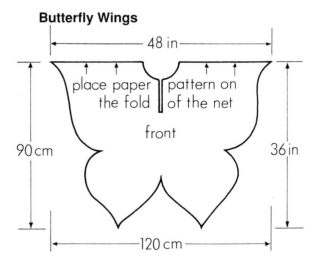

These butterfly wings can be made from approx 2 metres (2 yards) of dress net, width 136cm (54in). Decorate with a mosaic of crêpe paper pieces. If fluorescent net and crêpe can be found, the effect is particularly attractive.

Having first checked the measurements given against the child, draft and cut a paper pattern of the front of the butterfly as shown.

Cut a half circle for the neck, diameter 20cm (8in) in the centre of the shoulder line.
Fold the dress net double across the width. Pin the paper pattern on to the net, placing the shoulder line on the fold of the net. Cut out the butterfly shape and unfold. Cut an opening 18cm (7in) down the centre front.

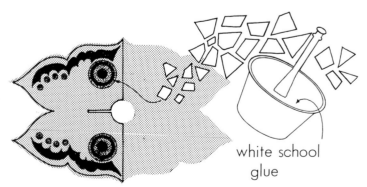

white school glue

Draw and colour the wing design on to the paper pattern and lay the front half of the net over the design. Cut up small pieces of crêpe paper of the required colours. Using the paper guide which will show through the net, children can stick the mosaic design on to the net wings. Keep lifting the net to prevent it from sticking to the paper below.

27

Underarm Wings
(photograph opposite)
These wings may be made from newspaper, crêpe paper or Vilene interfacing. They are best attached to a tight fitting T-shirt or leotard.

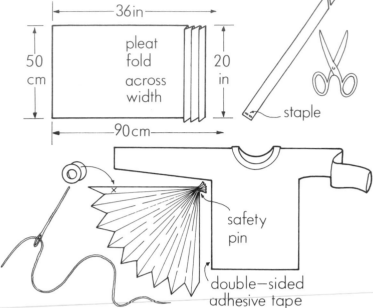

Mesh Wings
These are made from a pair of tights and two wire coathangers.

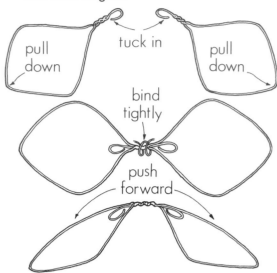

Re-shape both coathangers as shown. Tightly bind the hangers together at the neck with thin wire. Push the two wings forward.

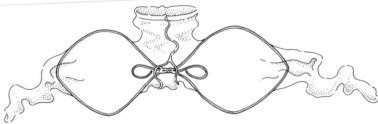

For each wing cut a rectangle 90cm x 50cm (36in x 20in) and pleat fold as shown.
Staple the bottom of the folded strip together and trim the top end to a point.
Attach the stapled end of the strip to the underarm of the T-shirt with a large safety pin. Fitting the T-shirt and wing on to the child, mark the wrist length along the top of the wing. Stick paper reinforcing rings each side of the wing at the mark and thread a length of elasticated thread through the rings. Tie the thread around the child's wrist.
The bottom of the wing can be secured to clothing with double-sided adhesive tape.

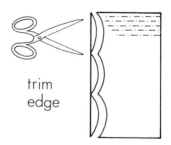

Bat wings can be cut from black heavyweight Vilene interfacing. Shape the edge of the flat wing as shown before pleat folding and stapling into position.

Carefully pull the tights over the wings so that the crotch is in the centre and the legs extend out each side.

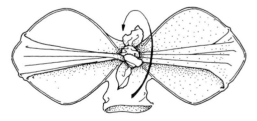

Pull both feet towards the centre back of the wings and knot securely. Wrap the waist around the knot tightly and secure neatly with a safety pin.

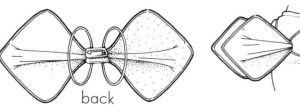

The wings are held in place with two loops of elastic through which the child puts his/her arms.

Wing instructions on these two pages, Owl Mask on page 32, Body Disguise on page 23

Transparent Insect Wings

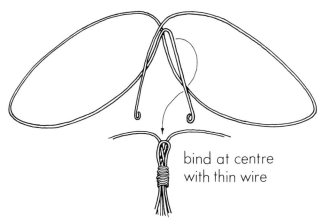

bind at centre
with thin wire

Cut a length of thick wire 240cm (96in) and bend as above. Secure the wing shape at the centre by tightly binding with thin wire. Stretch a length of kitchen clingfilm over each wire wing; it will stick to itself on the other side. The wings may be lightly 'veined' with coloured permanent markers.

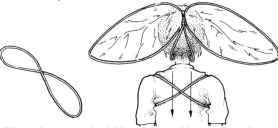

The wings are held in place with a twisted loop of elastic stretched across the shoulders. Slide the two wire wing supports behind the crossed elastic.

Quick Crêpe Wings

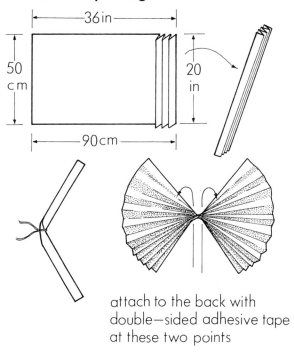

attach to the back with
double—sided adhesive tape
at these two points

Cut a 90cm (36in) length from a roll of crêpe paper. Pleat fold, and then twist the pleated strip at the centre, securing with an elastic band or thread. Allow the wings to open and attach to the back of the bodice with double-sided adhesive tape.

TAILS

Quick Cat's Tail

This is a simple paper tail; a more realistic tail is shown in the next column.

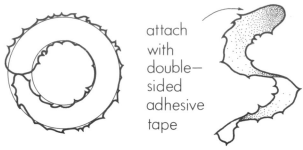

attach with double-sided adhesive tape

Draft a circle diameter 25cm (10in).
Draft a smaller circle diameter 15cm (6in).
Adapt the shape as above and cut out.

Lamb's Tail

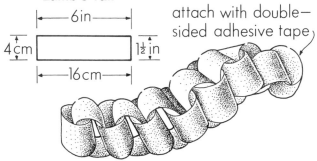

attach with double-sided adhesive tape

Cut links using the measurements given and construct a paper chain.

Pig's Tail

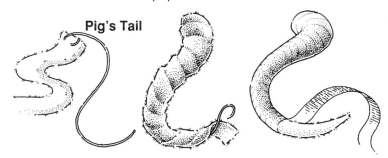

Using wire cutters, cut a length of plastic coated wire 25cm (10in) and curl into shape. Cut a strip of Terylene wadding 4cmx50cm (1½in x 20in). Loop the end of the wire into the wadding to secure it. Tightly bind the length of the wire with the wadding, securing at the other end by folding the wire over Cut a narrow strip of pink crêpe paper from the end of the roll and bind round the tail. Secure and neaten the ends with a rubber based glue.
Attach the tail with a large safety pin from inside the clothing.

Rabbit's Tail

This rabbit's tail can be made from crêpe or tissue paper, but the best material is Terylene wadding.

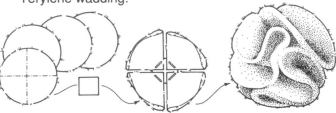

Cut four circles diameter 20cm (8in) from the chosen material. Cut a small square of thin card. Fold each circle into a quarter and staple on to the card.
Carefully open up each circle.
Attach the tail with a large safety pin or double-sided adhesive tape.

Cat and Mouse Tails

These tails are made from Terylene wadding. Colour is best applied with spray paint.

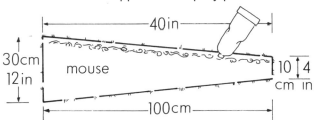

Cut the mouse's tail from wadding, using the measurements given. Apply rubber based glue along the top edge.

Roll the tail and hold in place with pins. Tie a length of thick thread round the wide end of the tail and wind tightly down the length as shown. Bind the tip, thread a needle and finish with a French knot. Remove the pins. Repeat for a cat's tail, using the measurements below.

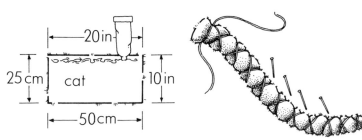

Bind the tail down to the bottom and then back up again, tying at the top.
Attach both tails with a large safety pin from inside the clothing.

Instructions on facing page

Cow's Tail
(photograph on page 49)
Use cheap taffeta or lining material which frays when torn into strips.

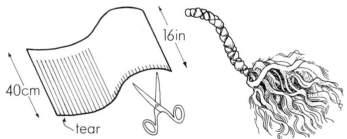

Find scraps of material approx 40cm (16in) in length. Snip along the bottom edge and tear into fringing. Roll the fringed scraps together. Bind the top half of the tail with thread as shown. Attach the tail with a large safety pin from inside the clothing.

Horse's Tail
(photograph on page 49)

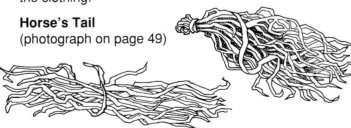

Use an assortment of materials, such as garden raffia, string, wool, strips of brown gummed paper, crêpe paper and torn lining fabric.
Cut the above into 90cm (36in) lengths. Secure round the centre with raffia. Fold the length in half and bind the top of the tail with raffia.
Attach the tail with a large safety pin from inside the clothing.

Fox's Tail
(photograph on page 49)

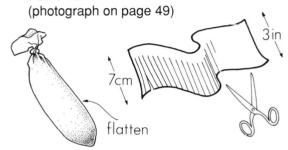

Stuff a black stretch pop sock with Terylene wadding or shredded paper. Knot the top of the sock and flatten into a tail shape.
Cut and fringe red, black and white strips of crêpe paper.

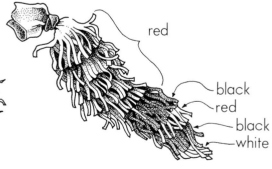

Starting from the bottom of the tail, glue the coloured strips round the sock as shown above. Glue the tip of the tail into a point. Attach the tail with a large safety pin from inside the clothing.

31

MASKS

Though masks can be effective and entertaining for the onlooker, they can be both frightening and impractical for the child wearing them. So often, masks impair vision and prove difficult to secure. On the following pages are some ideas which should overcome these problems.

Headband Masks
(photographs of owl mask on page 29, and bear mask on page 53)
This method of constructing a mask can be adapted to a wide variety of animals and birds. The mask can be cut out of any substantial paper and decorated in many different ways.

If many similar masks are required, it is worth making a card template; the children can then trace and cut around their own mask before decorating it. Features may be drawn, painted, printed or glued, though it is unwise to saturate the paper with too much wet paint or glue. Round adhesive labels are always useful for eyes.

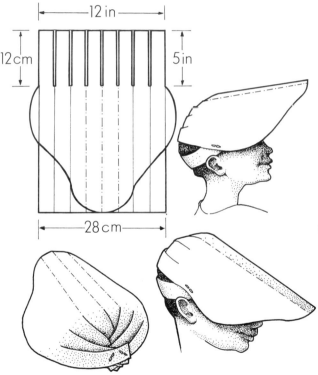

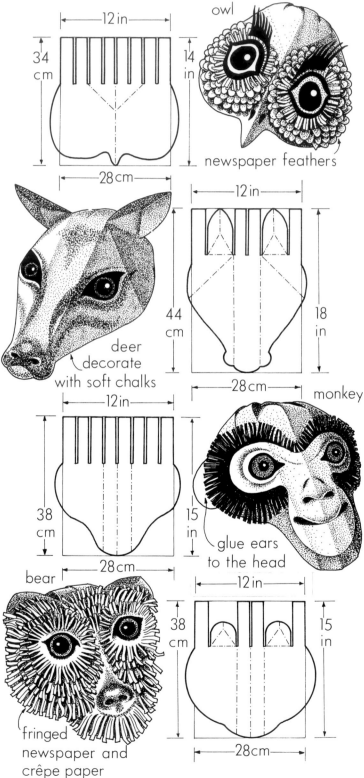

owl

newspaper feathers

deer
decorate
with soft chalks

monkey

glue ears
to the head

bear

fringed
newspaper and
crêpe paper

The shape is based on a rectangle, the top of which is cut into eight strips. The measurements are given above, though the overall length of the mask will depend on the animal or bird depicted (see next column). The strips are stapled together and the finished mask is secured on to a paper headband which has been fitted to the individual child's head. The angle is such that if the child holds his head up, he can see under the mask; if he looks down, the mask is completely visible. The child does not look through the mask.

Masks on Sticks

These masks are constructed from stiff corrugated cardboard secured on to a garden stick.

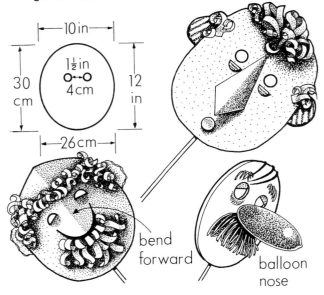

Cut an oval shape from the cardboard. The measurements given relate to the masks in the photograph. However, the mask can be of any size, though the eye holes will need to be approx 4cm (1½in) apart and cut by an adult. Children will enjoy creating different characters. A three-dimensional face can be achieved by folding the basic mask forward or by gluing shapes on to the mask. The widest possible range of materials can be used for decoration, including papier mâché.

A variation on the previous mask: remove the centre of the mask, allowing the child's face to show through.

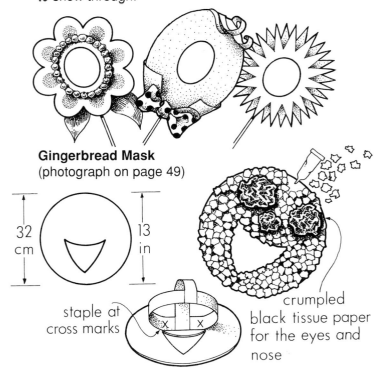

Gingerbread Mask
(photograph on page 49)

Cut a circle diameter 32cm (13in) from stiff corrugated cardboard. Remove a large smiling mouth shape from the bottom half, allowing the child to see through the hole. Crumple small pieces of brown tissue paper, and glue on to resemble gingerbread texture. Fit a headband to the child and add a crossband over the top of the head. Staple to the mask as shown.

Eye Masks

(photograph on page 27)
Children's plastic sunglasses make an ideal base for eye masks. Many children will have a pair, and if not, they can be bought cheaply from newsagents and toy shops.

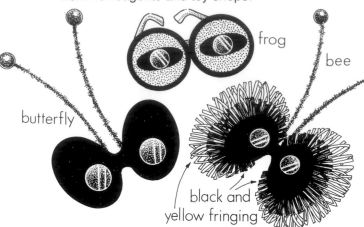

Trace round the outer shape of the sunglasses on to the mask paper so that the eventual eye holes line up with the lenses. Draw and cut the mask shape, removing the eyeholes, and decorate as wished. Antennae can be made from long pipe cleaners with craft balls on top.
Secure the mask on to the glasses with small pieces of Blu-Tack.

Headbands

Headbands have been included in the mask section as they can provide a base for features and, in particular, for ears.
Headbands should be cut from thick paper 4cm x 60cm (1½in x 24in), and secured firmly at the back of the head with double-sided adhesive tape, or staples inserted with the smooth edge next to the hair.

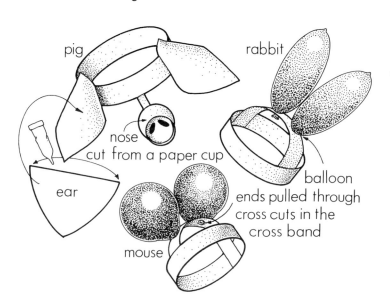

Bird Heads

(Photograph of penguin and albatross heads on page 55)

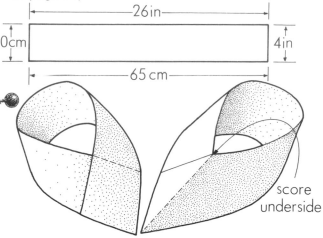

Cut a strip of paper of the required colour 10cm x 65cm (4in x 26in). Curve the strip round and secure as shown with glue or double-sided adhesive tape. Scoring the paper from behind, make a sharp fold centre front for the beak line.
(This simple headdress could be made by children and used when working on 'The Penguin's Question' on page 55.)

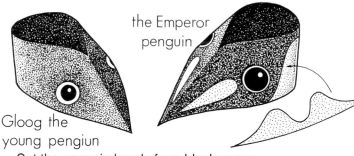

Cut the penguin heads from black paper using the measurements given.
Decorate the Emperor penguin with the distinctive orange markings and complete all the heads with eyes, using adhesive labels.

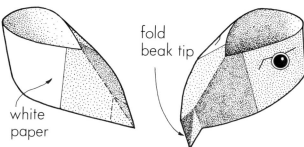

Cut the albatross head from orange paper. Cover the feathered section with white paper. Score the end of the beak to make a diamond shape. Fold the beak tip downwards and complete the head with eyes, using adhesive labels.

34

THE PLAY AREA
Some ideas to encourage improvisation and transformation

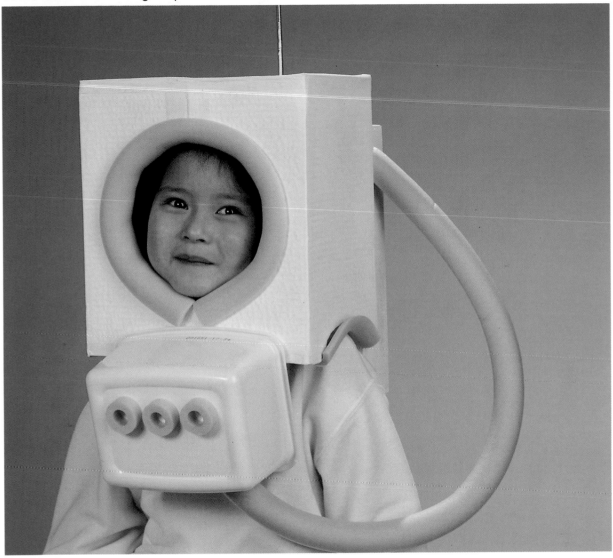

See instructions for spaceman's helmet on page 15

Small groups of children can use the play area in turn. Preparation for imaginative play in that corner can be made with the whole class, for instance by reading a story, extending topic work, and gathering their suggestions. Children can make their own labels and notices for games within.

Goldilocks and the Three Bears
Read the story to the class. Put into the play area a table, three chairs, bowls, spoons and three cushions as beds, for the children to lay out as if in the Bears' cottage. Then they can act the story as they wish.

Café or Diner
Find the class's experience of eating out, if any, and what they like best to eat. Let them set out a table and chairs to serve food to each other, or collect, pay and take food to the table. Provide plastic plates, cups, cutlery and toy money.

Shop
Set up a small shop with till and shelf. In class, discuss and contrast corner shops and big supermarkets. Collect empty packets and plastic bottles as goods for sale. Provide real or toy money to pay at the till, and carrier bags to pack the shopping. Children can shelf fill and arrange the shop, enjoy counting, serving and buying.

House

Talk about different sizes and shapes of families, to prepare children to play mums and dads, with babies, brothers, sisters, grandparents, uncles, aunts, lodgers, at home. Provide cushions or rugs for beds, if possible, as well as table and chairs for meals, as above.

Travel Agent

Explain to the class how the agent telephones to check that there is room on coaches, aeroplanes, in holiday camps and hotels. Children can make posters of holidays, other countries, trains, ships. Supply a table, chairs and telephones. Inside the travel shop children can buy tickets for holidays and outings. They can make their own, or use a book of raffle tickets.

Space Ship or Rocket

All try out a countdown to Blast-off. Talk about landing and meeting strange creatures from outer space, then returning to earth.

Puppet Theatre

By rigging up a curtain across the entrance, the play area can be transformed into a puppet theatre. Puppeteers can practise, then act to the rest of the class. (See following pages.)

Rain Forest

Decorate the play area with creepers of rope, its leaves and flowers painted and cut out by the children. Net hung over the top can also be decorated with leaves. Children's pictures of animals and birds can be pinned up. They can sit round a 'fire' of twigs, cooking food. If practicable, face paint can be used.

Fairy Tale Castle

The simplest cardboard cut-out battlements can transform the play area into a castle.
Many fairy tales take place in castles, and children can enjoy play-acting in their own style the stories which have been read to them. Try 'Beauty and the Beast', 'The Princess and the Pea', 'Rapunzel', 'Puss in Boots' and 'The Sleeping Beauty'.

Doctor's Surgery

Talk about the people who may be in a doctor's surgery, and what may be wrong with them. Practise coughing, limping, baby-crying, looking ill. Provide telephones, pencils, prescription pads, bandages, scales, or pretend scales, a toy stethoscope.
Children can be the doctor or nurse, or patients waiting their turns to be seen.
If there is any space nearby, the doctor's surgery can be extended into a hospital, and 'patients' can be visited in 'beds' outside the play area.

End of term party

Not all children will have birthday parties, so draw out some ideas of parties. Provide balloons, and wrapping paper for them to wrap and unwrap little pretend presents.
Talk about special food. Inside the play area, feasting can be imaginary; or a group can be hosts and prepare 'fairy' sandwiches (hundreds and thousands on bread and butter) and arrange crisps and biscuits on plates, then bring them out to the class, and all play a party game, such as Musical Bumps.

PUPPETS

Talking Egg Boxes
Use a cardboard eggbox with a hinged lid.

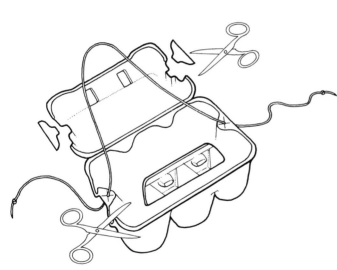

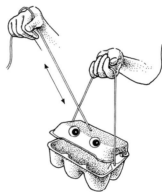

The puppet is held by the loop in one hand while the other hand opens and closes the mouth. If wished, paint the eggbox and then decorate with features, hair and hats.

It might be helpful if the puppets are designed in pairs, so that the children can decide what sort of conversation the puppets might have, and how different their voices might sound.

Cut off the front 'catching' flap and trim along the sides of the lid as shown.
Cut a length of string approx 80cm (32in). With the help of a thick needle, thread the string through the cross marks, making a long loop with a knot at either end.

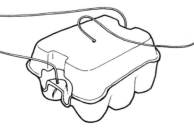

Cut a shorter length of string, knot the end and thread through the centre of the lid.

thread
string through hats

PUPPETS

Stick Puppets

Using a plain piece of paper, the child draws round his/her spread hand, omitting the thumb.

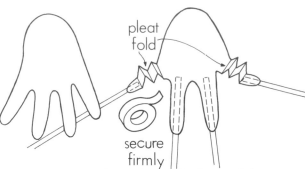

This cut out shape forms the base of the puppet, the two centre fingers representing the legs. Pleat fold the two outer fingers, giving greater movement to the arms. Position narrow straws to the back of each leg as shown and secure firmly. Secure a straw to the end of each arm.

Decorate puppets with paper, doilies and crayons.

Nursery rhymes might be a good starting point in giving ideas for characters and the movements they might make (see page 40 onwards). If a large mirror is available, the children could experiment in front of it to gain the full effect of their puppets' actions.

Flower Pot Puppets

For each puppet you will need a plastic flowerpot, diameter 15cm (6in).

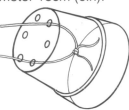

Cut a length of thin string 130cm (50in) and thread through the holes in the bottom of the flowerpot. Knot the ends to make a loop by which the puppet is held.

For each leg, cut a strip of thick paper 4cmx50cm (1½in x 20in).

For each arm, cut a strip of thick paper 3cmx20cm (1inx8in).

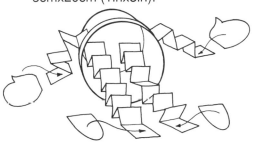

Pleat fold the strips of paper and secure the legs inside the bottom of the flowerpot, and the arms on the outside, as shown. Hands and feet may be added.

Decorate the puppet as wished.

By experimenting with the loop of string, these puppets can dance, jump and sit down. A piece of music might well provide inspiration for how the puppets could be used.

Older children might like to add a second loop of string connected to the hands to give a greater variety of movement.

Flower Pot Puppets

Sock Puppets

Different socks suggest different creatures. Here are some variations on a familiar puppet. It is worth remembering that eyes, whether they are buttons, beads or craft balls, can be given greater expression or highlights with the addition of sticky labels.

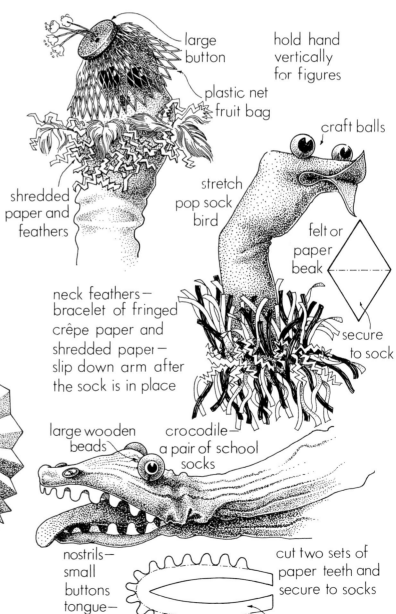

large button

plastic net fruit bag

hold hand vertically for figures

craft balls

shredded paper and feathers

stretch pop sock bird

felt or paper beak

secure to sock

neck feathers —
bracelet of fringed crêpe paper and shredded paper —
slip down arm after the sock is in place

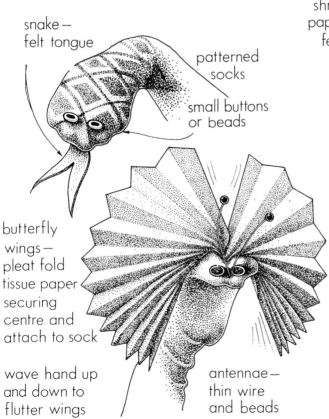

snake —
felt tongue

patterned socks

small buttons or beads

butterfly wings —
pleat fold tissue paper securing centre and attach to sock

wave hand up and down to flutter wings

antennae —
thin wire and beads

large wooden beads

crocodile —
a pair of school socks

nostrils —
small buttons
tongue —
felt

cut two sets of paper teeth and secure to socks

colour gums pink

39

Acting in Nursery Rhymes

Children can join in chanting these rhymes with the teacher, learning to act to the words as they speak.

SOLO ACTING

Let each child find a space to play the part;
if necessary, some ideas can be initiated by
the teacher.

Little Jack Horner

Sat in a corner,
Eating a Christmas pie.
He put in a thumb
And pulled out a plum
And said 'What a good boy am I.'

The North Wind does blow,

And we shall have snow,
And what will poor Robin do then, poor thing?
He'll sit in a barn,
And keep himself warm,
And hide his head under his wing, poor thing.

Pussy-cat, Pussy-cat, where have you been?

I've been up to London to look at the Queen.
Pussy-cat, Pussy-cat, what did you there?
I caught a little mouse under her chair.

ACTING IN FOURS

Make quartets.

(Three kittens and mother cat)
Three little kittens, they lost their mittens,
And they began to cry,
'Oh, mother dear, come here, come here,
For we have lost our mittens.'
'Lost your mittens! You naughty kittens,
Then you shall have no pie.'
'Miaow, miaow, we shall have no pie.'

Three little kittens, they found their mittens,
So they began to cry,
'Oh mother dear, come here, come here,
For we have found our mittens.'
'Found your mittens? You good little kittens,
Now you shall have some pie.'
'Prr, prr, now we shall have some pie.'

ACTING IN TWOs

Choose partners.

Little Miss Muffet

Sat on a tuffet,
Eating her curds and whey.
There came a big spider,
Who sat down beside her
And frightened Miss Muffet away.

Little Miss Tucket

Sat on a bucket,
Eating some peaches and cream.
There came a grasshopper,
Who tried hard to stop her,
But she said 'Go away, or I'll scream.'

Lucy Locket lost her pocket,

Kitty Fisher found it.
Not a penny was there in it,
Only ribbon round it.

ALL CLASS ACTING TOGETHER

Little Bo-Peep has lost her sheep,
And can't tell where to find them.
Leave them alone, and they'll come home,
Wagging their tails behind them.

Little Bo-Peep fell fast asleep,
And dreamt she heard them bleating.
But when she awoke, she found it a joke,
For they were still a-fleeting.

Then up she took her little crook,
Determined for to find them.
She found them indeed, but it made her
heart bleed.
For they'd left their tails behind them.

She heaved a sigh and wiped her eye,
And ran over hill and dale, O,
And tried what she could, as a shepherdess
should,
To tack to each sheep its tail, O.

Instructions for making Bonnet on page 13

ALL CLASS ACTING TOGETHER

Sing a Song of Sixpence,
A pocket full of rye.
Four and twenty blackbirds,
Baked in a pie.

When the pie was opened,
The birds began to sing,
Wasn't that a dainty dish
To set before the King?

The King was in his counting house,
Counting out his money.
The Queen was in the parlour,
Eating bread and honey.

The Maid was in the garden,
Hanging out the clothes,
When along came a blackbird,
And pecked off her nose.

They made such a commotion,
That Little Jenny Wren
Flew down into the garden,
And stuck it on again.

Mary had a little lamb,
Its fleece was white as snow,
And everywhere that Mary went
The lamb was sure to go.

He followed her to school one day,
That was against the rule.
It made the children laugh and play
To see a lamb at school.

And so the teacher turned him out,
But still he lingered near,
And waited patiently about
Till Mary did appear.

And then he ran to her and laid
His head upon her arm,
As if to say, 'I'm not afraid,
You'll keep me from all harm.'

'What makes the lamb love Mary so?'
The eager children cry.
'Oh, Mary loves the lamb, you know,'
The teacher did reply.

41

Assemblies
Some guidelines

A class contribution to an assembly will be more enjoyable for participants and audience if mime and acting are included. The ideal is to involve the whole class, however modestly.

Without doubt, the simplest dressing-up, such as masks or tails, will turn a performance into a treat.

The following suggestions can be adapted and expanded to match the abilities and ages of classes.

PRESENTING NURSERY RHYMES (see also page 40)

Sing a Song of Sixpence. This can be mimed by a King, Queen, the blackbirds (at first in a big heap as the pie, and all with small black wings, see page 29). The Maid can wear an apron and Jenny Wren can have little brown wings. The whole class can act and speak, or one section recite in chorus.

Sung action rhymes, such as 'Here we go round the Mulberry Bush' are easy to prepare.

NUMBER RHYMES
Divide the children into groups, who can act out the rhymes together.

Groups of six can act:
Five currant buns in a baker's shop,
Round and fat with a cherry on top.
Along came a boy with a penny one day,
Bought a currant bun and took it away.
Four currant buns....

Groups of ten can be sausages:
Ten fat sausages frying in the pan (Twice)
One went pop and the other went bang.
Then there were eight fat sausages,
Frying in the pan.
Eight fat sausages...

Or ten children can be green bottles:
Ten green bottles hanging on the wall, (Twice)
And if one green bottle should accidentally fall,
There'll be nine green bottles hanging on the wall.
Nine green bottles hanging on the wall...

As many elephants as you wish...
One elephant went out to play
Upon a spider's web one day.
He found it such enormous fun
That he called for another elephant to come.

STORIES
Use those which children can animate. Here are two of Aesop's Fables for the whole class to act.

The Fox without a Tail. The teacher can read the story and point out its moral. All the class make and wear fox tails (see page 31), except the one who catches his tail in a trap and has only a stump left.

The Shepherd Boy and the Wolf. This story, with its moral of telling the truth, needs the class to take the parts of the shepherd boy, his flock of sheep (see page 30) and a group of villagers.

Instructions for making Crowns on page 13

RELIGIOUS STORIES
These can be told in the same way.

The Good Samaritan has a smaller cast: the man who fell among thieves, the thieves, a priest, a Levite, a Samaritan and an innkeeper. This mime can lead to a parade of people who help us in daily life, dressed-up and perhaps wearing names: nurse, fireman, policeman and so on.

JOINING IN THE STORY, with actions and sounds effects
Tell a simple story, of a family holiday or day out, having divided the class into groups, to represent each character: Dad - clearing throat, 'Now then'; Mum - rocking baby, 'There there'; Boy - kicking imaginary football, 'Goal!'; Girl, skipping with imaginary rope, 'Jump!'; Baby - crying; Dog - barking; Cat - miaowing; Car - engine sound, made by everyone.

Practise the sounds, then as the story is told, each group steps forward or stands up (if practicable) and makes its sound and action whenever mentioned, and 'the Family' causes everyone to react.

RELIVING HISTORY
Fact, as well as fiction, can be presented dramatically, as a class shares its interests and enthusiasms with the rest of the school. Part of a family's 'history' might be shown, with the collaboration of a parent and grandparent. Weddings and other celebrations in different cultures can be re-created by the children. The scope is limitless.

Older children can use more ambitious material from their own writing, and later sections of this book.

Acting in Stories from Around the World

THE THIEF WITH CLEAN HANDS
A Chinese story to mime

Cast: Magistrate Chen; Constable; nine Suspects and one Thief; four Constable's men; crowd of spectators (rest of class).

Props: Chair for Constable and Chen, and mime everything else.

Diagram of cast arrangement:

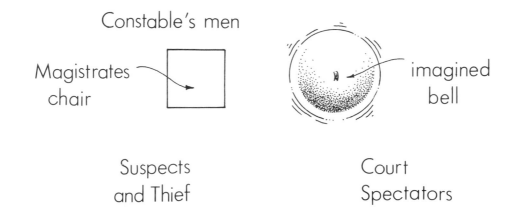

Narrator: **A long time ago, in China, there was a big robbery. The police constable's men brought to the court all the people he thought might be thieves.** *(His four men bring the nine suspects and the thief on stage from left and right, and sit them in front of him. When questioned, each stands up in turn and shakes his head.)*

The Constable asked them a lot of questions, but he could not find out who the thief was.

'I give up,' said the Constable. 'I'll have to ask Magistrate Chen to help me. He is so clever, he will find out the truth. *(He goes off to get Chen.)*

Chen was so wise, people came to hear him act as a judge in the Court. *(Chen enters, sits in chair, and spectators sit to watch, at right.)*

Chen did not ask any questions. He said to the Constable's four men: 'In the temple of the great Buddha there is an old bronze bell. Bring it here to me, with four fire pots.' *(They bow and go off.)*

The men brought the firepots and the bell, and hung the bell up on poles. *(They mime this.)*

Then Chen lit the four fire pots and let them smoke by the bell for a long time. *(Mime this.)* **When the fires had died down he asked the men to cover the bell with a big cloth, so that it looked like a tent.**

Chen spoke to the suspects. 'This bell from Buddha's temple will tell us which of you is a thief. If an innocent man rubs the bell it will make no sound. But if a thief rubs the bell it will chime at once, and then we shall all know who is guilty.' *(Suspects and crowd react with excitement. Chen bows and prays with hands together and upright in front of the bell, then leads each suspect to it in turn. He watches while each one puts a hand under the cover to rub the bell. In each case there is silence. The crowd sighs each time.)*

Instructions for making Chinese hats on page 12

After each suspect rubbed the bell there was no sound at all. But Chen held on to the last suspect.

'Here is the thief,' he said.
'No, I'm not,' shouted the man. 'The bell didn't ring when I touched it.'
'No, it didn't,' shouted the crowd *(angry).* 'It's not fair.'
'Wait a moment,' said Chen. 'Please take the cover off the bell.' *(Constable does so. Everyone reacts with surprise.)*

Everyone was surprised to see that the bell was covered with black soot, except for hand marks round the rim.

'Now look at this man's hands,' said Chen. *(He makes the man show his hands.)* Only *his* hands are clean. The others all have soot on theirs. *(Other suspects look at their hands.)* Only the thief did not dare to touch the bell, because he thought its chime would give him away. Take him away to prison, Constable. All the rest of you are free to leave the court.'

(Crowd applauds. Thief is taken away. Chen bows and goes off.)

FURTHER ACTIVITY
Try making chiming bells from earthenware flower pots. Suspend them with thick string, secured at the hole by a knot. Sound them with a wooden spoon or pencil, and demonstrate that they will chime only when free to vibrate.

HOW DOG BECAME MAN'S FRIEND
An African story to mime

Starting-point:
- Explain that a jackal is in the wild dog family, about as big as a fox, living in Africa and Asia.
- Each child stands in a space, and pretends to be and move like a dog - ask for suggestions from the children.
- Read the story aloud slowly, and let the children respond by acting as the dog.
- The story can be read again, with the children in trios, as Dog, Man and Jackal.

NARRATOR: **A long time ago, in Africa, Dog and Jackal lived together in the wild bush country. Every day they went out hunting for food.**

One day, they caught no food. In the wild bush that night a cold wind was blowing.

'I'm so cold,' said the Dog, 'and I'm hungry too.'

'Lie down and try to go to sleep,' said Jackal. 'Then we'll go hunting again in the morning, when it's light.'

'But I'm too cold to sleep,' said Dog. 'My fur coat isn't as thick as yours.' He looked across the windy wild bush. 'What's that red light over there?'

'It's a Man's fire in his village,' Jackal told him.

'Will you go and get me some fire?' asked Dog. 'Then I'll be warm.'

'No, the Man might catch me,' said Jackal. 'Go and get it yourself.'

'I'm too scared,' said Dog. And he curled up small and tried to go to sleep. But he was still shivering, cold and hungry.

He started thinking about the Man's fire, and wondered if there were any bones left on the ground from the Man's meal.

Dog sat up and said to Jackal: 'I'm going to see that fire and find some bones. If I don't come back by the morning, call me, so I can find you.'

Then Dog crept off to the fire in the Man's village. He could smell cooking, and started looking for bones. But the Man heard him, and came out of his hut, waving his spear. Dog crouched down, frightened.

'What have you come here for?' the Man asked fiercely.

'Just to get warm by your fire,' said Dog. 'I won't hurt anyone in your village. When I'm warm, I'll go back to the bush.'

'All right,' said the Man. 'You can stay here till you are warm.'

'Thank you, kind Man,' said Dog, and sat by the fire, chewing a bone he had found.

In a few minutes, the Man came out from his hut again.

'You must be warm by now,' he said.

'Can I stay a bit longer?' asked Dog. 'I'm nearly warm.'

'All right,' said the Man.

So Dog chewed his bone, and had a little sleep by the warm fire. In a few minutes, the Man came back.

'You must be warm by now,' he said.

'Yes, I am warm,' said the Dog, 'but I do not want to leave you and your warm fire and go back to the cold wild bush. Can I stay with you? (Dog begs.) I can help you hunt for birds and animals. And I promise I will never steal your chickens.'

'All right,' said the Man. 'I will let you stay to keep warm by my fire, and let you eat the leftovers from my meals, if you will work for me and do what I tell you.'

'Thank you, Master,' said Dog, and walked behind the Man into his hut.

So Dog went to live with the Man, and Jackal went off with a pack of other jackals, howling round the wild bush country.

FURTHER ACTIVITY

Ask children to draw different breeds of dogs which they know. Talk about working dogs: for the blind and the deaf; police dogs; sheep dogs; St. Bernard dogs used in mountain rescue.

THE GINGERBREAD MAN
An English story for acting in the round, with class chorus

Starting-point:
- Read the story of *The Gingerbread Man,* so that the class can pick up the repeated chorus lines, encouraging them to join in.
- Discuss - and the children try out the movements of the characters:

  - Gingerbread Man, running. Does he run with stiff arms and legs?
    The class can choose.
  - Old Woman, slow on her feet.
  - Cow, chewing cud.
  - Horse, pawing the ground.
  - Farmer, digging.
  - Fox creeping, then swimming.

- Let the class divide into pairs and decide the best way to pretend that the Fox eats up the Gingerbread Man, tipping him over his head. Each pair demonstrates and the class decides on the best way to act each part.

Cast: Old Woman, Gingerbread Man, Cow, Horse, Farmer, Fox.

The rest of the class becomes the Chorus, sitting in front of the acting space in a group. This is arranged so that the Gingerbread Man can run round in a circle.

Prop: A chair.

Diagram of cast arrangement:

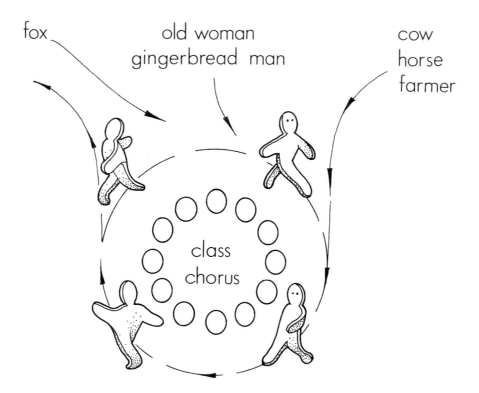

TEACHER/NARRATOR: **Once upon a time, an Old Woman was making gingerbread. She rolled it out to make into biscuits, and she cut one out in the shape of a boy.**

'I'd like to have a Gingerbread Boy,' said the Old Woman. And she put him in her hot oven to cook. (*She puts a tray on chair seat, as oven, and shuts the door. Gingerbread Man is crouched behind.*)

In three minutes the Gingerbread Boy shouted: 'I'm ready now. Come and let me out.'

48

Instructions for making Gingerbread mask on page 33. Instructions for making tails on page 31

The Old Woman was so surprised she opened the oven door at once. Out jumped the Gingerbread Boy. *(He jumps out to side of the chair.)*

'You're cooked already, Gingerbread Boy,' she said.

'I'm not a boy. I'm a man,' he said.

'You look good enough to eat. When you're cool I'll eat you up.'

(CHORUS)   **'Oh no, you won't,' said the Gingerbread Man.
'Run, run, as fast as you can,
You can't catch me,
I'm the Gingerbread Man.'**

(He runs round the class Chorus. Old Woman chases him, but does not catch him. Gingerbread Man comes running round and meets the Cow, entered from right, and chewing cud.)

Then he met a Cow. The Cow said 'Moo-moo-moo, you look good enough to eat. I think I'd like to eat you up. Just stop a minute, Gingerbread Man.'

(CHORUS)   '**Oh no I won't**,' **said the Gingerbread Man.**
                    '**Run, run, as fast as you can...**' **etc.**

(He avoids the Cow's attempts to bite at him, and runs round, chased by Cow. Gingerbread Man comes running round and meets Horse, entered from right, pawing the ground, and possibly swishing his tail.)

Next he met a Horse. The Horse said 'Neigh-neigh-neigh, you look good enough to eat. I think I'd like to eat you up. Just stop a minute, Gingerbread Man.'

(CHORUS)   '**Oh no, I won't**,' **said the Gingerbread Man.**
                    '**Run, run, as fast as you can...**' **etc.**

(He avoids the Horse's attempts to bite at him, and runs round, chased by Horse. Gingerbread Man comes running round and meets the Farmer, entered from right, and digging at the earth.)

When he met a Farmer, the Farmer said, 'Hello, hello, hello, you look good enough to eat. I think I'd like to eat you up. Just stop a minute, Gingerbread Man.'

(CHORUS)   '**Oh no, I won't**,' **said the Gingerbread Man.**
                    '**Run, run, as fast as you can...**' **etc.**

(He avoids the Farmer's attempts to grab him, and runs round, chased by Farmer. Gingerbread Man comes running round and stops, dismayed.)

Now when the Gingerbread Man came running to a river he had to stop, because he could not swim. Just then a Fox came creeping along *(from left)*. **He thought the Gingerbread Man looked good enough to eat, but he did not say so. He said 'Would you like to cross the river?'**

'Yes please,' said the Gingerbread Man.

'Then jump on my back and I'll carry you,' the Fox told him.

The Gingerbread Man jumped on the Fox's back, and he began to swim across the river.

'Climb on to my neck,' said the Fox. 'Then you won't get wet.' The Gingerbread Man climbed on to the Fox's neck.

'Climb on to my head,' said the Fox. 'The water is very deep.' When the Gingerbread Man was on his head, the Fox said, 'Lean over on my nose, then you'll stay dry.'

But as the Gingerbread Man leaned over, the Fox opened his mouth and went 'Snip-snap', and he ate him all up.

(CHORUS)   '**And that was the end of the Gingerbread Man.**'

FURTHER ACTIVITY
● Make Gingerbread Men in dough, pastry or Plasticine.
● Cut out from pleat-folded paper a row of Gingerbread Men.

THE GREEDY CAT

An Indian story, to join in by miming

Starting-point:
- Read the story straight through to the children, relaxed and with their eyes shut, imagining it happening.

- Arrange positions. Cat and Parrot 'centre stage'; Old Woman, Man and Donkey enter from left; the procession enters from the right. All the eaten characters will sit or crouch behind the Cat, ready to come out later.

- Before acting the story, everybody works out and practises movements of characters:
  - the Cat: reaching out and grabbing food, packing it in behind him.
  - the Parrot: small birdy steps.
  - the Old Woman: bent, holding shawl round her shoulders.
  - the Old Man: bent and slow moving.
  - Donkey: kicking out at intervals (one or two children).
  - King and Bride: regal movements, as if wearing robes.
  - Soldiers: marching in time together.
  - Elephants: one or two children per elephant, right arm for swinging trunk.
  - Crabs: crawling sideways.

- Children take up positions and act in the story, told aloud again.

NARRATOR: **A long time ago, in India, a Cat and a Parrot were friends. Every day they had dinner together, and they took turns to cook the meal.**

When it was his turn, the Cat cooked a small piece of fish and a small bowl of rice. (They eat, Cat grabbing, Parrot pecking.) **The Parrot was still hungry after that meal.**

When it was his turn, the Parrot cooked five hundred spicy cakes. (He carries them in front of Cat.) **He gave four hundred and ninety-eight cakes to the Cat, and kept only two for himself.**

(Enter Old Woman, who watches at left.)

51

Now this Cat was greedy. He swallowed all the four hundred and ninety-eight spicy cakes. *(He pushes them into his mouth.)* Then he looked at the Parrot's two spicy cakes and said, 'I'm still hungry.'

The Parrot told him, 'All YOUR cakes have gone.'
'Then I shall eat you up,' said the Cat. And so he did.

An Old Woman shouted at him, 'You greedy Cat, eating your friend the Parrot!'

'I'm still hungry,' said the greedy Cat. 'Yummy-yum, into my tum, I'm going to eat you up.' And so he did. *(He grabs her, and pushes her behind him. Enter Old Man, left.)*

Then along came an Old Man with his Donkey. 'Keep clear of my cross Donkey,' he said to the Cat, 'or he might kick you.'

'He won't have a chance,' said the greedy Cat. 'I'm still hungry. Yummy-yum, into my tum. I shall eat him up, and you as well.' So he did.

Next, along came a wedding procession. *(They enter in order.)* There was a King, his bride, six marching Soldiers and four Elephants, swinging their trunks.

'Keep clear of my Elephants, Cat,' said the King, 'or they might tread on you.'

'They won't have a chance,' said the greedy Cat. 'I'm still hungry. Yummy-yum, into my tum, I'm going to eat you all up.' *(He grabs and pushes them behind him, in turn.)* So he ate up the King and his Bride, the six marching Soldiers and the four Elephants.

By now, the greedy Cat was so full he could hardly move. *(Enter Crabs.)* He saw two Land Crabs crawling along. 'Watch out, Cat,' said the Land Crabs, 'or we will nip you with our pincers.'

'You won't have a chance,' said the greedy Cat. 'I'm still hungry. Yummy-yum, into my tum, I'm going to eat you up.' And so he did. *(He grabs and pushes them behind.)*

Now inside the Cat there was such a crowd of people and animals, the crabs could hardly crawl. But they said to each other, 'We must get out of here.' So they began to nip a hole in the Cat. They nipped and nipped until it was a very big hole. *(They all come out in order.)*

The Crabs jumped out of the Cat's tummy. Then the King climbed out, holding his Bride's hand. The Soldiers marched out. The Elephants came out, waving their trunks. The Old Man led his Donkey out. The Old Woman hobbled out and shook her fist at the greedy Cat.

Last of all came the Parrot, holding two spicy cakes.

After that, the Cat only ate fish for his dinner - and the Parrot ate up the two spicy cakes for his tea.

FURTHER ACTIVITY
- Make fish from cardboard, with pieces of silver and gold paper glued on for scales.
- Make real cakes.

THE BIG BEAR-CAT
A story from Scandinavia, made into a play, for reading and acting

Bear Mask instructions on page 32, Furry Feet on page 25

Starting-point:
- The simple dialogue can be photocopied and read or learnt by the speakers; **or,** children can improvise their own dialogue, once they have grasped the story.
- Explain that trolls are dwarfs or imps in Scandinavian folk tales. All the class can be trolls, and pool ideas on their 'bad behaviour'. They may also practise wicked expressions and have a growling contest to choose the loudest growler for the Bear-cat; then decide how the trolls might squeak.

Cast: Man, Bear, Halvor, Wife, Three Children, Trolls (rest of class).
Props: Probably more scope for movement if no furniture or props are provided.

THE BIG BEAR-CAT

(Enter Man, left, with Bear)

MAN:	**The King will be very pleased when I give you to him as a present. You are such a beautiful big white bear.** *(He pats Bear, who grunts.)* **But we won't reach the King's palace tonight. I think we should find shelter** *(Bear nods.)* **I'll try this house.** *(He knocks at door. Halvor opens the door a little.)* **Please can we come and stay at your house? It is so cold outside.**

HALVOR:	**I'm sorry, no.**
MAN:	**But it's so cold. And I think it's going to snow. May we come in?**
HALVOR:	**I'm sorry, no.**
MAN:	**If you haven't a room, we'll sleep by your fire.**
HALVOR:	**I'm sorry, no.**

MAN:	But it's Christmas time. Don't you want to help us?
HALVOR:	I'm sorry, no. You see, every Christmas time a crowd of wicked trolls comes into our house and goes wild. They spoil everything. My wife and three children can never sit down with me to enjoy our Christmas dinner.
MAN:	We're not scared of trolls. They won't worry us. Please let us in and we'll sleep on the floor.
HALVOR	All right, but I have warned you. *(Opens door.)*
MAN:	*(going in and crossing to right with Bear)* **What a lovely hot fire. You can sleep here, Bear. I'll stay by you.** *(Bear lies down. Man sits on floor by him. Wife comes in, carrying things, followed by three children. All mime putting dishes on table.)*
CHILD 1:	What a big bear.
CHILD 2:	Will he bite?
CHILD 3:	Can I stroke him?
MAN:	He won't hurt you. He's a friendly bear. *(They kneel down and pat Bear.)*
WIFE:	**Please come and share our Christmas dinner, if you wish and if...**(*Running sound of all trolls running on the spot off stage.)* **Oh dear.** *(They come running on from each side and push and climb and gobble food from the table. Bear and Man are calm, but the children frightened.)* **Come on, we'll have to shelter in the wood shed.** *(She takes them off protectively. Halvor shrugs helplessly at Man and follows them. After more fooling, one troll goes up to Bear, bends and stares at him cheekily. Then he goes and gets a sausage from the table, comes and waves it in front of Bear's nose. As he does so, other trolls quieten and watch.)*
TROLL:	**Pussy, pussy, have a sausage to eat.** *(As Bear opens his mouth to eat it, Troll snatches the sausage away and laughs. Bear stands up and growls loudly, lumbers round and chases trolls out of the house, from under the table, from in corners, and so on.)*
MAN:	**Well done, Bear-Cat! They didn't know who they were teasing. Have a sausage.** *(Calls)* **Halvor, bring your wife and children back. Then we can eat what's left.** *(Family returns cautiously.)*
WIFE:	Have they all gone?
CHILDREN:	What a brave Bear!
HALVOR:	We must clear up the mess.
WIFE:	**There is still some food left in the kitchen.** *(The family mimes clearing up, and the wife brings in more food.)* **Come and eat.** *(They all sit at table, and the Bear sits on the floor by Man and is fed by him. Children start yawning and their mother takes them off to bed. They kiss Bear goodnight and go off, followed by Halvor. Bear and Man go to sleep on the floor. Halvor returns after a short pause.)*
HALVOR:	I hope you slept well.
MAN:	**We did. Thank you for having us to stay.** *(Gets up.)* **Now I must take my Bear to see the King.**
HALVOR:	**Goodbye, and thank you for sending those wicked trolls away.** *(Man leads the bear off.)*
HALVOR:	**When Christmas comes again I'll have to think what to do, so we can eat our Christmas dinner in peace every year.** *(He goes off. Pause, then he comes back, carrying a chopper.)* **It's nearly Christmas again. I must chop some extra wood.** *(Goes left stage, and mimes chopping wood.)*
TROLLS:	*(Mocking, calling voices)* **Halvor, Halvor, Halvor.**
HALVOR	What is it? Who's out there in the woods?
TROLLS:	Is your big white cat still with you?
HALVOR:	**Yes, she is,** *(smiling to himself)* **and she has seven big kittens now, all of them much fiercer than she is. So what do you think of that?**
TROLLS:	We'll never ever, never ever come to your house again.
HALVOR:	**I don't think they will, thanks to the Bear-Cat. I must go and tell my family.** *(He goes off.)*

FURTHER ACTIVITY

● Make up a big white Bear's slow dance.
● Make Christmas decorations from straw, as in Scandinavia, remembering Jesus in the manger.

THE PENGUIN'S QUESTION
A play in the round for the whole class to read and act

Instructions for penguin and albatross masks on page 34

Starting-point:
● Show pictures of penguins, then all class practise waddling with small steps. Try tying legs together under the knees with a scarf or band. Practise limited movements of the flippers out from the body with straight arms and, perhaps, screeching.
● Practise the flapping of the Albatross's big wings and the Puffin's small wings, and the Polar Bear's lumbering walk. Try out the Seal's swimming and throwing pebbles, the Sealion's singing and the balancing of a stone.
● Try making simple headdresses to be worn (see above).

Cast: Narrator (or all class take these lines); Gloog (a Penguin); Albatross; Flontarol the Seal; Sea-Lion; Polar Bear; Mrs. Puffin; Punig (a penguin friend); Emperor Penguin; Other Penguins (the rest of the class).

Diagram of cast's positions and suggested movement (can be a circle or an oval):

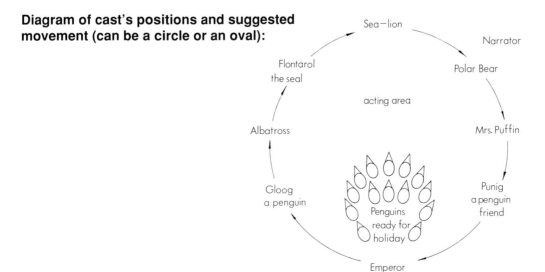

Arrange the class in a circle, as above. Gloog works his way around, with the action mostly taking place 'centre stage'.

NARRATOR:	*(Gloog stands up and waddles to the centre.)* **Gloog is a young penguin who lives in a very cold country. One morning, a big white bird flies down.** *(Albatross flaps by Gloog.)*
ALBATROSS:	**Who are you?**
GLOOG:	**I'm a penguin.**
ALBATROSS:	**What's that?**
GLOOG:	**It's a bird.**
ALBATROSS:	**Then where are your wings?**
GLOOG:	**I haven't any wings. I have these flippers instead.** *(Flaps them.)*
ALBATROSS:	**You're not a proper bird like ME, the astonishing Albatross. I can fly for miles without getting tired.** *(He flaps his wide wings.)*
GLOOG:	**You'll blow me away!**
ALBATROSS:	**They are strong wings, much better than your feeble flippers.**
GLOOG:	**But I can slide on the snow on my tummy. I push myself along with my flippers and feet. I race with my friend Punig.**
ALBATROSS:	**You'd better ask him why you can't fly like me.** *(He flies away with big flapping movements, to left, and lies as if asleep.)*
NARRATOR:	**Gloog goes down to the sea to find some fish for breakfast.** *(Gloog waddles about.)* **Flontarol the Seal comes floating towards him on a sheet of ice.**
GLOOG:	**Do you know, Flontarol, why penguins don't have wings for flying?**
FLONTAROL:	**I've no idea. I only need a strong tail for steering, and my fins. They're much more use than wings. Just watch me throw these little stones with my fins.** *(He does this while Gloog watches.)* **Don't you bother about wings. Come and have a ride to the big ship. Much better than flying.**
NARRATOR:	**So they floated out to a big ship, then swam round it listening to music till Gloog felt tired and swam back to shore.** *(Class hums while Gloog swims in centre, then over to the Sea-lion. If wished, the other penguins can transform themselves into waves, swaying.)* **A large Sea-lion, Flontarol's cousin, was lying at the edge of the sea.**
SEA-LION:	**What can I do for you, young penguin?**
GLOOG:	**I was just going to...**
SEA-LION:	**I know. You would like to hear me sing.** *(He rolls round on his tail, honks and groans.)* **Oooh, Oh, Oing.**
GLOOG:	**Thank you very much, Mr. Sea-lion, but I wonder if...**
SEA-LION:	**You want to know how I balance stones so cleverly. I put my nose down to the snow, lift a stone and hold it like this. Have a try.** *(He demonstrates.)*
GLOOG:	**I don't think penguins' noses are good at balancing things. I don't mind that, but I do wonder why I don't fly.**
SEA-LION:	**Sea-lions never fly.** *(He dives swoosh into the water and back to his place.)*
NARRATOR:	**Gloog began to climb the cliff nearby, still looking for his friend Punig. He balanced himself with his flippers, up and up, till he found a cave.** *(Gloog climbs.)*
GLOOG:	*(calling down into cave)* **Is anybody at home?**
POLAR BEAR:	*(in deep voice)* **Yes, I'm at home. Who's there?**
GLOOG:	**It's me, come to ask a question.**
	(Polar Bear lumbers out to the centre.)
GLOOG:	**Please, I wonder if you know, Mr. Polar Bear, why I have flippers instead of wings?**
POLAR BEAR:	**Perhaps they are small wings, and will grow if you eat lots of fish.**

GLOOG:	No, big penguins have flippers too, and I want to know why we don't fly.
POLAR BEAR:	It's much better to walk or gallop over the snow, like me. And if I come to thin ice, I lie down flat and slide.
GLOOG:	That's clever, but it's not flying. I'll try sliding down the cliff again. *(Slides on tummy. Mrs. Puffin, a small fat bird with wings, moves centre.)*
MRS. PUFFIN:	*(calling)* Gloog, Gloog.
GLOOG:	Hello, Mrs. Puffin. Perhaps you could help...
MRS. PUFFIN:	I am very busy, and I need your help. Can you count to ten?
GLOOG:	Yes, I can, but...
MRS. PUFFIN:	*(snapping her deep beak)* Then just stand there and count by the water. I can get ten fish in my beak for my children, and I want to make sure that I have ten, so they can have five each. *(She fishes with beak in water.)*
GLOOG:	One, two, three, four, but I wonder...
MRS. PUFFIN:	You talk too much. Count!
GLOOG:	Five, six, seven. What a neat row!
MRS. PUFFIN:	I said count!
GLOOG:	Eight, nine, ten. *(Mrs. Puffin closes her beak and flies away.)* Oh dear, she's gone before I could ask her anything. *(Punig waddles centre; Gloog bows and Punig bows back.)* Oh, Punig, I've been looking everywhere for you, to ask why I don't have wings. The Albatross said I wasn't a proper bird. Nobody seems to know why we penguins don't have wings.
PUNIG:	It's really a secret, but the biggest Emperor Penguin told me. Millions and millions of years ago, we used to fly in the air. But penguins decided they wanted to spend more time in the water, to catch more fish.
GLOOG:	A good idea.
PUNIG:	So they thought flippers would be better than wings.
GLOOG:	And they grew flippers?
PUNIG:	Very very slowly, their wings changed to flippers. They became better at swimming. And they flew under water.
GLOOG:	I'd like to find the Albatross and just tell him about us penguins.
PUNIG:	We can ask the chief Emperor Penguin about that. He's taking a party of young penguins over the ice hills for a holiday. We might catch him. *(Gloog and Punig waddle round and meet Emperor, followed by all the other penguins. Gloog and Punig bow.)*
EMPEROR:	Good afternoon to both of you.
GLOOG:	Please may we ask you about wings, sir?
NARRATOR:	And they told him all about the Albatross.
EMPEROR:	I'll soon speak to the Albatross. We'll call on that rude bird. *(He makes a trumpeting noise and walks quickly, followed by Punig, Gloog and all the other penguins. They find the Albatross fast asleep. He soon wakes up when all the penguins screech.)* We thought you would like to know that penguins don't have wings because we don't want them any more. We gave them up millions and millions of years ago. We find flippers much better.
ALL OTHER PENGUINS:	*(waving flippers)* Much better.
ALBATROSS:	*(nervously)* Oh I see. I think I'd better be fly-...I mean, going now *(flaps wings)*.
GLOOG:	*(calling)* Remember, penguins don't fly because they don't want to fly any more.
ALL OTHER PENGUINS:	Any more.
GLOOG:	It's taken me a long time to find that out. Perhaps I need a holiday too.
PUNIG:	May we come with you, sir?
EMPEROR:	The more penguins the better.
ALL PENGUINS:	*(parade around outside the circle and then go)* Off we go, over the snow. We can slide on the ice and fly through the water, without any wings at all. Off we go, over the snow...

MR TULIP IN THE HAT SHOP

● This story is for miming practice, and enjoyment. Some classes will need a read-through first, to take in the story. Then each child takes the part of Mr Tulip, using what space is available. The teacher can tape the story ahead, at a pace to allow the action, and lead the acting for children to join in.

The children can wear their own dressing-up hats as a fireman, a jockey and so on.

NARRATOR: Mr Tulip was an odd job man. One day, he went out cleaning. He was going to clean a hat shop. There were so many hats that Mr Tulip thought it was a wonderful shop.

'I'm so glad you like my shop,' said the shopkeeper. 'As I want to sell lots of hats, I want my shop window to be smart and clean. Then people will look in it. They'll see my hats, then they'll buy some hats. While I'm away I want you to clean the window and sweep the floor. Then I can come and put the hats on show.'

'Certainly, sir,' said Mr Tulip. 'Just leave it to me.'

Mr Tulip waved goodbye to the shopman and started to sweep the floor. But then he saw a fireman's helmet. And he felt he just had to try it on.

As soon as the hat was on his head Mr Tulip thought he WAS a fireman, at his fire station, having a quiet cup of tea. Suddenly a bell rang, and Mr Tulip slid down a pole, pulled on his fire clothes and jumped into the fire engine. He drove the engine to the fire. Everyone had to get out of his way.

Mr Tulip stopped the fire engine and went to look at the fire. There was a lot of smoke, so Mr Tulip climbed up a ladder to have a look around. There was nobody there. He had to get rid of the red hot flames. Mr Tulip squirted a hose up on to the roof, then on to the door. There wasn't much smoke left. The red hot flames had all gone away. And that was the end of the fire. Mr Tulip rolled up the hose and put it on to the engine. Then he set off back to the fire station. He wanted to finish his cup of tea.

Mr Tulip had been day-dreaming about being a fireman. But he had to start cleaning the shop. He started to sweep the floor again. But then he saw a spaceman's helmet. And he felt he just had to try it on.

As soon as the helmet was on his head, Mr Tulip thought he WAS a spaceman. And he set off in his rocket to have a quick look at the moon. When the rocket was ready he had to hold tight. It was Blast-off. He was getting up speed. He was leaving the earth. The rocket was going at top speed. Although it was time for his dinner, Mr Tulip couldn't eat it off a plate. He had to suck it out of a tube!

Next he was landing on the moon. So he went off for a walk. He felt very bouncy on the moon. It was so soft and dusty under his boots. Then Mr Tulip went back to his rocket, and turned it straight back towards Earth. He wanted to sleep in his own bed, and was soon on his way back home.

Mr Tulip had been day-dreaming about being a spaceman. But he had to start cleaning the shop. He started to sweep the floor again. But then he saw a jockey's cap. And he felt he just had to try it on.

As soon as the cap was on his head Mr Tulip thought he WAS a jockey with his horse Neddy. He wanted to try to win a race. He was hoping his horse would come in first. The horses were all standing in a line. Mr Tulip was ready. With a one and a two and a three and a BANG, they were off!

Mr Tulip was doing well. He thought he was winning. He'd never gone so fast before. But poor old Neddy, there was a hedge! Mr Tulip fell off. Neddy should have jumped a bit higher, but Mr Tulip felt Neddy's legs and was glad that he hadn't hurt himself.

Mr Tulip had been day-dreaming about being a jockey. He had hardly done ANY cleaning in the shop.

'What have you been doing?' asked the shopman, coming in the door. 'Nothing looks any cleaner to me. I want to sell the hats. And my window's still dirty.'

But Mr Tulip pointed outside the window. There was a big crowd of people who had been watching him.

'We want to see some more hats,' they said. 'He's only shown us a few.'

'Come right inside,' said the shopman. 'Don't bother about any more cleaning, Mr. Tulip. Just sell all the hats you can.'

Mr Tulip let people try on lots of hats. He seemed to choose the right hat for each person. As soon as a man put on a hat he wanted to buy it. Mr Tulip kept on selling hats until there was not one left in the shop.

The shopman was delighted. 'You may not be very good at cleaning, Mr. Tulip,' he said, 'but you have been very good at selling hats.'

Improvisation can be continued: Chef's hat, diver's helmet, policeman's helmet, explorer's pith helmet.

THE STAR'S STORY
A mimed Nativity play

Cast: Star, Gabriel, Mary, Joseph, First Innkeeper, Second Innkeeper, Innkeeper's wife, four Shepherds, one Shepherd Boy, four Angels, three Wise Kings, with page boys. Give everyone a part by including more shepherds and angels.

Narration: by teacher, or good readers in class, solo or in chorus.

Props: Manger and low stool; standing blocks for Star; Gabriel and the holy family; baby lamb and sheep (toys or hand-made models).

● Make a tape of the story in advance, reading slowly, to allow time for the action to take place.
● Read 'The Star's Story' aloud to all the class. Then explain that they will supply the 'pictures' by acting. Show Christmas cards of Old Masters, or old manuscript illustrations of the Nativity.
● Arrange the cast to left and right of the stage or acting space and at the back of the hall behind the audience. If there are no curtains or side classrooms, waiting characters will have to stand at the sides. Those at the back will enter down a central gangway.

Cast arrangement at the beginning of the play:

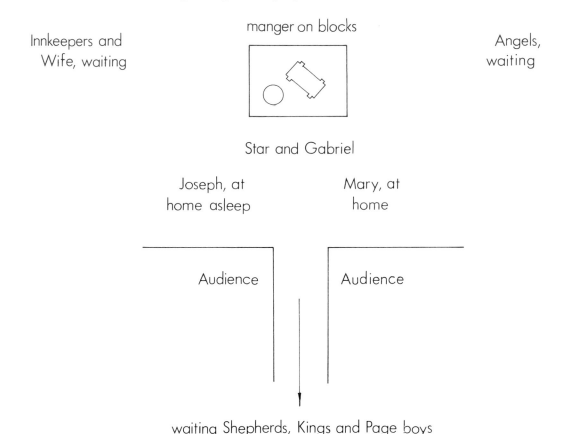

Play tape with your familiar voice, and so be free to direct the characters to learn their cues, move on and off and act their parts to the words as they practise. The Star can carry a torch.

THE STORY

NARRATOR:
The Star's Story. I am the Angel Gabriel's star.
A long time ago, my angel flew with me to Mary's house in Nazareth. *(Gabriel and Star 'fly' across stage to right front, where Mary is found standing.)*

My light was so bright that Mary hid her eyes. *(Mary covers her eyes at first.)*
'Do not be afraid,', said Gabriel. *(Gabriel kneels, and is seen in profile.)* **'God has chosen you to be the mother of his Son.'**

Mary looked upset. 'But I am going to marry Joseph.'

'I shall tell Joseph about this as well', said Gabriel 'and he will understand.'

'Then I will do what God wishes,' said Mary, 'and wait for my baby.' *(She bows her head.)*
Next we flew to Joseph's house. *(Gabriel and Star fly up stage and across to left front, where Joseph is lying asleep. He wakes.)*

'Joseph', said Gabriel, 'do not be afraid. Mary will have God's Son and you will be his father on earth. When he is born, call him Jesus.'
'I will do what God wishes,' said Joseph. *(He nods and bows to Gabriel, then goes offstage.)*
Some time later, Gabriel told me that Joseph and Mary had to go to Bethlehem. *(Gabriel and Star are front stage. Mary crosses stage behind them, to join Joseph.)*
'Help them,' he said. 'Shine on their way so that their donkey does not stumble and fall.'

(Star leads. Mary walks slowly, supported by Joseph, around the stage. Mary is very weary.)
I gleamed in the sky as Joseph led the donkey with Mary on his back for seven days and seven nights. *(Innkeepers and wife come on stage and stand in line, wife nearest the front.)* It was late in the day when we came to Bethlehem. I could see that Mary was tired.
'I need to rest,' she told Joseph. 'My baby will soon be born.'

(Star is behind Mary and Joseph upstage as Joseph mimes knocking, moving towards front stage.)
Joseph knocked on a door. 'Please have you room for us to stay?'
(Innkeeper shakes head.)
'No room here,' he was told.
(Another innkeeper shakes his head, after more knocking.)

They tried many places, but all of them were full.

It was almost dark when we found an inn. I shone so brightly on Joseph and Mary that the innkeeper's wife could see how worried they were, and she was very sorry for them.

'We have no room in the inn', she said, 'but you could shelter in our stable, with the cows and the donkey. It is warm and dry there.'
So I lit them into the stable.

(Mary, Joseph and the innkeeper's wife are at left front stage. The wife takes Mary by the arm and leads her to the manger, centre mid-stage. She uncovers the manger and a stool for Mary, who sits with her back to the audience. Then she lifts the baby from the manger, and shows him to Joseph before putting him back.)

When the baby Jesus was born they wrapped him up and put him in the manger for a cradle. The animals hummed him a lullaby. I glowed for Jesus until he fell asleep.

(Gabriel watches to one side. Star stands on block behind the manger.)

(Mary rests on stool and Joseph stands beside her, hand on her shoulder.)

While Joseph and Mary rested, I hurried away across the black sky to tell Gabriel that the baby was born.

(Gabriel and Star meet front stage, then fly down gangway to back of hall, where shepherds are waiting.)

And he flew to some fields where shepherds were taking care of their sheep, so that wild animals did not hurt them. The shepherds blinked at my bright light. *(Shepherds hide their eyes, frightened.)*

'Do not be afraid,' said Gabriel. 'I have come to bring you good news. A Saviour has been born in Bethlehem. Follow my star and you will find him.'

(Music of 'While Shepherds watched their flocks by night' with everyone in cast humming, as the shepherds process down the central gangway, following the Star and Gabriel to the manger. Extra shepherds can sit in front of the audience. Angels enter from right with upraised arms.)

Other angels clustered round me and sang with Gabriel 'Glory to God in the highest. Peace on Earth, goodwill to men.'

Then the angels went back to heaven. *(Angels go off slowly, with wings folded or hands across chests. One shepherd stays.)*

One shepherd stayed with the sheep and the others followed me to the stable. *(Shepherds follow Star to the manger, where they kneel, and shepherd boy gives a lamb.)*

A shepherd boy took a little lamb as a present, which made the baby smile. *(Gabriel and Star behind manger. Shepherds, smiling, move off stage left, to await tableau.)*

Padded medieval hat, instructions on page 11

When the shepherds went back to their sheep they were very happy. They told everyone the good news we had given them about the baby Jesus.

Next Gabriel told me to go to a far country where wise men were looking at the sky. *(Star and Gabriel go down the gangway to the Kings and pages.)* 'You, my star, will be a special sign to lead them to Jesus.'

Three wise Kings were watching the sky and waiting. When they saw me they said, 'How wonderful! It has come at last. This must be the brightest star in the world. Now we can follow it and find the baby King.'
(The Kings are delighted, arms outstretched.)

I led the way as they rode on their camels for many days and many nights. *(Kings and pages process slowly down the gangway after Star and Gabriel. Music of 'We three Kings of Orient are', everyone humming.)*

Then I glittered over the stable and lit their way inside.
(Kings move to the manger.)

'We have come to visit the baby King,' said one of them.
'He will not be like other kings,' said Mary, 'I think he will be a King in heaven.'
The three Kings knelt down and gave the baby presents of gold, frankincense and myrrh.
(Each kneels in turn and puts a present by the manger.) Then the Kings went back to their far country, very pleased with all we had shown them. *(They go off right.)*

(Gabriel smiles approvingly upon Star, who stands behind the manger.)

Gabriel said, 'Well done, my star. Stay with this holy family.'
(Exit Gabriel right, to heaven.)

Every night I glimmered a little for the baby Jesus, so that he was never in the dark, and when Mary was strong again we set off. I led Joseph with Mary and the baby all the way back home to Nazareth.

(Star comes forward and leads Mary and Joseph across left to Nazareth. Mary holds the baby, Joseph holds the baby lamb. They go off to the left.)

(Star stays left front stage.)

Today I am a star still shining in your sky. When it is dark in the winter, if you look out of your window and find the brightest star, you will know who I am...and you will remember the story of Christmas, with Mary, Joseph and the baby Jesus, Gabriel and other angels, the innkeepers, the shepherds and the three wise Kings.

(Star gestures the characters back as they are mentioned, to form a tableau of the Nativity. As this happens, the cast begins singing 'Away in a Manger'.)

Away in a manger, no crib for a bed,
The little Lord Jesus lay down his sweet head.
The stars in the bright sky looked down where he lay,
The little Lord Jesus asleep on the hay.

The cattle are lowing, the baby awakes,
But little Lord Jesus no crying he makes.
I love thee, Lord Jesus, look down from the sky,
And stay by my side until morning is nigh.

(Mary takes the baby from the manger and cradles him in her arms. Cast and audience all sing:)

Be near me, Lord Jesus; I ask you to stay
Close by me for ever, and love me, I pray.
Bless all the dear children in thy tender care,
And fit us for heaven, to live with thee there.

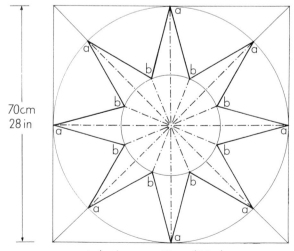

70cm
28 in

outer circle diameter 70cm (28in)
inner circle diameter 30cm (12in)
score aa lines on front of card
score bb lines on back of card

The Star headdress

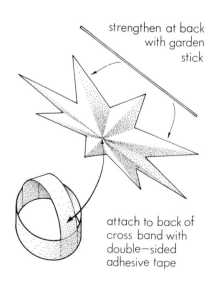

strengthen at back
with garden
stick

attach to back of
cross band with
double-sided
adhesive tape

GOODBYE TO A GREEDY DRAGON

A play for the whole class

Cast (in order of appearance):
Announcer
Wise Woman
Village people, men and women
Dragon (two people or more)
Carpenter
Carpenter's boy
Cook
Drummer
Soldiers
Village children, boys and girls
(The numbers in the groups can be adjusted to include everyone in the class.)

Dragon's Costume: Our dragon is based on nylon fruit netting which can be bought cheaply by the metre/yard from garden centres. Once cut to the required length, it is decorated with circles of crêpe or tissue paper and ribbons of crêpe paper knotted through the netting. A row of crêpe rosettes can mark the spine. The head is constructed from thin card using an enlarged version of the headband mask (page 32). The chosen number of children form the body by supporting the netting with padded garden sticks, two of which protrude through the netting to provide the base for the pleated crêpe paper wings.

Props: Food for the dragon, black book, hammer, nails, blocks, saucepan lids, a drum, a sword.

Scripts: Photocopied scripts can be colour marked to help children find and read, or learn, their own lines.

Scene: Outside a village. At left back, a cave's mouth or cave from which the dragon can emerge. To the front right of acting area, a chair for Wise Woman, who sits reading from a large black book. (A large pot with paper hollyhocks could suggest her cottage garden.)

ANNOUNCER: **We present 'Goodbye to a Greedy Dragon'. The scene is outside a village, a long time ago.**

(Wise Woman comes and sits outside on a chair, and begins to read her book, facing the audience. One villager is unpacking a giant rope of sausages from a basket, and is at once joined by four others, carrying baskets of food.)

VILLAGER 1: **It's getting past a joke trying to feed a dragon. He had eight loaves yesterday; pounds and pounds of potatoes and carrots; three dozen eggs, their shells and their boxes.**

VILLAGER 2: **Hunks of meat; strings of sausages.**

VILLAGER 1: **And not a grunt of thanks. Where is all this going to end?**

VILLAGER 2: **I'm sure he's eating more every day.**

VILLAGER 3: **Perhaps we should stop giving him so much.**

VILLAGER 4: **But then he would come into the village and grab it himself. Just imagine him tramping all over our little gardens.**

VILLAGER 5: **Smoking his way into our kitchens and shops. No thank you!**

VILLAGER 1: **But he is so greedy. And what does he do for us, when we give him all this food?**

VILLAGER 5: **Nothing.**

VILLAGER 2: **He is only a big fat dragon, and we're waiting on him as if he were   king.**

VILLAGER 3: **Perhaps we should tell him that we just can't afford...**

(Loud rumblings from cave. Villagers back away nervously as Dragon comes out slowly, flapping his wings, laying out his long tail to his satisfaction before bellowing slowly.)

DRAGON: **I am hungry. Where's my food?**

VILLAGER 1: **Here it is, Dragon.** *(Pushing it forward then retreating.)*

DRAGON: *(Picking it up and pushing it into his cave)* **Not much here, is there?**

VILLAGER 2: **All we can manage, Dragon.**

VILLAGER 3: **That would last us for days, Dragon.**

DRAGON: **Just a few tit-bits to me. You had better bring some more later. This just isn't enough for a marvellous dragon like me. After all, I am your guest!**

VILLAGER 4: **But we didn't invite you to come from the Land of the Dragons. And you do eat so much. We'll be running short ourselves any day now.**

DRAGON: **That's your problem! When I'm hungry, I need food.**

VILLAGER 5: **But Dragon.** *(Dragon disappears into the cave, with a flip of his tail.)* **It's no good. He won't listen. What can we do?**

VILLAGER 1: **He'll have to go.**

VILLAGER 2: **But how can we get rid of him?**

VILLAGER 3: **Tell him he's got to go.**

VILLAGER 4: **You try. He'd just burst into flames. You know what dragons are.**
VILLAGER 5: **More like greedy pigs, if you ask me.**

(Growl from within the cave. The sound may be improved by using a cardboard tube as an amplifier.)

VILLAGER 1: **I know. Come over here. I've got an idea.**

(The villagers huddle right, and in a stage whisper Villager 1 continues)

VILLAGER 1: **We must have a plot. He's much stronger than any of us, so we can't force him. We'll have to trick him.**
VILLAGER 2: **Easier said than done. I'd be scared.**
VILLAGER 4: **So would I. He could blow us over with his hot breath, or knock us over with his big wings.**
VILLAGER 3: **Why don't we ask the Wise Woman? She might have some ideas.**

VILLAGER 5: **Yes, let's go now and ask her advice.**

(They cross to right hand corner, and, when they speak to her, Wise Woman turns to them.)

VILLAGER 1: **Wise Woman, we have come to ask you for help. This Dragon!**
VILLAGER 2: **He's eating so much.**
VILLAGER 3: **More every day.**
VILLAGER 4: **There'll be no food left for us soon.**
VILLAGER 5: **He's getting fatter and fatter. But we're getting thinner and thinner.**

ALL
VILLAGERS: **So, please, Wise Woman, what can we do?**

WISE
WOMAN: **He must be sent back to his Land of the Dragons. You're making him too comfortable here...**

ALL
VILLAGERS: *(protesting)* **But we....but you see....we're not....he's just...**

WISE
WOMAN: *(holding up her hand for attention)* **If you ask for advice, you must listen! You will have to frighten this dragon away.**

ALL
VILLAGERS: *(appalled)* **What, us? But how?**

WISE
WOMAN: **I will tell you. You see, I happen to know that dragons do not like loud noises. So you must frighten him away with noise.**

VILLAGER 1:   *(doubtfully)* **We could try, I suppose.**

WISE
WOMAN: **Remember, this dragon likes to sleep all day. You can spoil that peaceful sleep.**

VILLAGER 2:   **Thank you, Wise Woman. It's worth a try.**
(Wise Woman dismisses them by opening her book again, and the villagers leave at back right, discussing the problem as they go.)

(The dragon emerges from the cave, and, with appropriate actions, eats the enormous string of sausages.)

DRAGON: **Not bad for a little snack.**
(He curls up in front of the cave, left, and goes to sleep. Enter, cautiously, from right, Carpenter, in apron, with his boy, carrying block of wood, hammer and nails.)

CARPENTER: **Put it there, boy, by the dragon. Not his tail, his head! We're here to wake him up, remember.**
BOY: **Yes, sir.** *(Boy puts block by dragon's head and steps back nervously. Carpenter kneels and gestures to be passed the hammer, then the nails. He begins to hammer, speaking in time.)*

CARPENTER: **This should shift him. Break his slumbers. Hammer-bang. Hammer-bang. Hammer-bang.**
(Boy mouths silently with him, and jumps at the bangs.)

DRAGON: **Did I hear a tapping?** *(He rolls over and goes straight back to sleep.)*

CARPENTER: **I wasn't loud enough. He only woke up for a minute. We must get help. Go and fetch my friend, the cook, and tell him to bring some lids from his pots and pans. That should wake this sleepy beast. Hurry now!**
BOY: **Yes, sir.** *(He hurries off right.)*

(Carpenter walks all round dragon, looking closely.)

CARPENTER: **You're a great big fat, lazy old...**
(Dragon snores and he jumps back, alarmed)..**marvellous dragon.**

(Enter Boy, with Cook, in chef's hat, carrying saucepan lids, by their knobs, to clash like cymbals.)

COOK: **You need a bit of help to get rid of the dragon, I understand.**

CARPENTER: **Yes, he's not really as fierce as he looks, just greedy, you know.**

COOK: *(Standing further away from the dragon than the carpenter)* **I'll take your word for it. Will this do? Clisher-clash, Clisher-clash. Clisher-clash.**

CARPENTER: **That was excellent. Now, when I count three...One...Two...Three.** *(They make and say the sounds.)* **Hammer-bang. Hammer-bang. Hammer-bang. Hammer-bang. Clisher-clash, Clisher-clash. Clisher-clash. Clisher-clash.**

(Boy mouths and watches, fascinated. Dragon raises head, then rolls over and goes back to sleep.)

CARPENTER: **We still aren't loud enough. Go and get some soldiers, Boy. They can march up and down. That should wake him!**

(Boy runs off to the left to the waiting soldiers.)

COOK: **He only woke up for a minute. I suppose he's so full of our good food, he just wants to sleep all day.**

CARPENTER: **Well, he won't now. Here come the soldiers.** *(Enter soldiers, drilled, marching from left across the stage.)* **Now if you march right by the dragon, that should do the trick. Start stamping when I say 'three'.**

SOLDIERS: *(marching on the spot)* **Will this do? Stamper-stomp. Stamper-stomp. Stamper-stomp. Stamper-stomp.**

CARPENTER: **That's excellent. Now. All together. One...Two...Three.
Hammer-bang. Hammer-bang. Hammer-bang. Hammer-bang.
Clisher-clash. Clisher-clash. Clisher-clash. Clisher-clash.
Stamper-stomp. Stamper-stomp. Stamper-stomp. Stamper-stomp.**

(The Dragon raises his head.)

DRAGON: **Did I hear more tapping?** *(He rolls over and goes straight back to sleep.)*

CARPENTER: **We still weren't loud enough. He only woke for a minute.**

SOLDIER 1: **Why don't we get our drummer? He could make a noise to wake up this lazy creature.**

CARPENTER: **Yes, send for the drummer at once.**

SOLDIER 1: **Go and get our drummer, as quickly as you can.**
(A soldier runs off.)

SOLDIER 2: **Of course, we could kill the dragon for you, though he is rather large...and he does look a bit fierce to me. Also, I wouldn't really want to blunt my new sword on his thick skin.**

CARPENTER: **There's no need to do him any harm. The Wise Woman says he's only lazy and greedy. We just want to send him away, and stop him eating all our food.**
(Enter Drummer, with soldier marching, up on to the stage.)

SOLDIER 1: **We need some drumming to frighten this dragon, my man. Send him packing. Dragons hate noise, you see.**

DRUMMER: **Certainly, sir. Something like this?** *(Speaking and drumming)* **Booma-boym. Booma-boym. Booma-boym. Booma-boym.**

CARPENTER: **That's just right. Now, all together when I say Three. One...Two...Three.**

(They all make the noises and say the words.)

> Hammer-bang. Hammer-bang. Hammer-bang. Hammer-bang.
> Clisher-clash. Clisher-clash. Clisher-clash. Clisher-clash.
> Stamper-stomp. Stamper-stomp. Stamper-stomp. Stamper-stomp.
> Booma-boym. Booma-boym. Booma-boym. Booma-boym.

(The dragon gets up on his front legs.)

DRAGON: **Did I hear some tapping? I hope it's not going to get noisy round here.** *(He rolls over and goes straight back to sleep.)*

CARPENTER: **We were NEARLY loud enough. We just need to wake him up a bit more.**

DRUMMER: **We seem to be making a good noise to me.**

SOLDIER 1:   **But not quite good enough. Who would have the loudest voice to shout at the dragon?**

SOLDIER 3:   **You can shout quite loudly, sir, when you're marching on parade.**

SOLDIER 1:   **That's quite different.**

COOK: **Why don't we ask the children? They can make plenty of noise. And they're tired of the greedy dragon taking all their food.**

CARPENTER: **Excellent idea. Boy, go and fetch the children at once.**
(While the Boy fetches the children, the Carpenter officiously arranges the others round the dragon's sleeping form.) **We must make noise all round him. This really should do the trick.**
(Enter children, from right. One of them goes over and brings the Wise Woman with them.)

CARPENTER: **Now, children, we have a job for you to do. This dragon has to be sent back to the Land of the Dragons because he is eating us out of house and home.**
(Children nod and murmur agreement.) **You are to shout as loud as you can:
'Dragon, Dragon, go away!'
Perhaps you had better have a little practice first.
Now, when I say three, shout your loudest: One...Two...Three!** *(He conducts the children.)*

CHILDREN: **Dragon, Dragon, go away!**

(Wise Woman taps her walking stick in time, with approval.)

CARPENTER: **That's it. Now all together. One...Two...Three!
Hammer-bang. Hammer-bang. Hammer-bang. Hammer-bang.
Clisher-clash. Clisher-clash. Clisher-clash. Clisher-clash.
Stamper-stomp. Stamper-stomp. Stamper-stomp. Stamper-stomp.
Booma-boym. Booma-boym. Booma-boym. Booma-boym.
Dragon...Dragon...Go...A...Way!**

(The Dragon gets up slowly on front legs, then back legs.)

DRAGON: *(Bellowing)* **What is this horrible noise? What's going on around here? Can't a dragon have a bit of rest?**

CARPENTER: **I think we need a bit of help. Any children out there?** *(To audience)* **Try it out with me. Dragon...Dragon...Go...A...Way!**

CHILDREN IN
AUDIENCE: **Dragon...Dragon...Go...A...Way!**

CARPENTER: **Well done. Come on everybody. Once again. As loud as you can!**
               One...Two...Three!
               Hammer-bang. Hammer-bang. Hammer-bang. Hammer-bang.
               Clisher-clash. Clisher-clash. Clisher-clash. Clisher-clash.
               Stamper-stomp. Stamper-stomp. Stamper-stomp. Stamper-stomp.
               Booma-boym. Booma-boym. Booma-boym. Booma-boym.
               Dragon...Dragon...Go...A...Way!

(The Dragon hangs his head. All pause for breath and watch him.)

DRAGON: **I've had enough holiday. I'm going back to my job in the Land of the Dragons.**
               I'm afraid I'm too fat to fly by now. And I'm too fat to run either. But I'm going
               home. There's far too much noise around here for me.

(He lumbers off, and into centre gangway. He goes right through centre of the audience, as the others stand and watch him go, snorting and lashing his tail.)

CARPENTER: **Now we'll have enough to eat. In fact, I must admit that all this work has made**
               me hungry.

EVERYONE: **Me too. And me.**

WISE
WOMAN: **Then let's all go home and have a big tea.** *(Slowly, with satisfaction)* **It isn't every**
               day that we say 'Goodbye' to a greedy dragon!

(They process out after the dragon, in order. When the Carpenter has said his 'hammer-bang' four times, the Cook joins in and they all follow, saying their parts until they are out of the back door of the hall. The children's rhyme changes:)

CHILDREN: **Dragon, Dragon, go away,**
               DON'T come back another day!

(The Wise Woman completes the procession, tapping in time with her stick.)

For details of further Belair publications,
please write to: Libby Masters,
BELAIR PUBLICATIONS LIMITED,
Albert House, Apex Business Centre,
Boscombe Road, Dunstable, LU5 4RL.

For sales and distribution (outside North America)
FOLENS PUBLISHERS
Albert House, Apex Business Centre,
Boscombe Road, Dunstable, LU5 4RL.
United Kingdom.

For sales and distribution in North America and South America,
INCENTIVE PUBLICATIONS,
3835 Cleghorn Avenue, Nashville, Tn 37215.
USA.

For sales and distribution in Australia
EDUCATIONAL SUPPLIES PTY LTD
8 Cross Street, Brookvale, NSW 2100.
Australia